Macmillan Junior Mathematics

2

Consultant: **Edith Biggs**
Chief author: **Melvyn Nolan**
Assisted by Jacqueline Dineen

ST. MARTIN'S C.E.
MIDDLE SCHOOL
ASHLEY ROAD, EPSOM

TEACHER'S NOTES

Macmillan Education

Text © Edith Biggs and Melvyn Nolan 1985
Illustrations © Macmillan Education 1985

All rights reserved. No reproduction, copy or transmission
of this publication may be made without written permission.

No paragraph of this publication may be reproduced, copied
or transmitted save with written permission or in accordance
with the provisions of the Copyright Act 1956 (as amended).

Any person who does any unauthorised act in relation to
this publication may be liable to criminal prosecution and
civil claims for damages.

First published 1985
Reprinted with revisions 1986

Published by
MACMILLAN EDUCATION LTD
Houndmills, Basingstoke, Hampshire RG21 2XS
and London
Companies and representatives
throughout the world

Printed in Great Britain by R J Acford, Chichester

ISBN 0–333–36961–0

Designed by Peter Lawrence, Oxprint Ltd

Contents

Page

iv   Introduction
vi   Scope and sequence chart

1   Number
6   Area
9   Mass
13   Number
19   Shape
24   Length
26   Time
28   Number
32   Volume and capacity
35   Area
38   Number

43   Shape
48   Length
52   Number
55   Time
58   Volume and capacity
61   Number
65   Mass
69   Shape
72   Number
75   Area
77   Time

Introduction

This series follows the Infant/First School level of *Macmillan Mathematics*. Although both series have common aims, each can be used independently.

The components

The materials are provided in four levels – one level for each year in the Junior School:

Level One   Pupil Book 1A
Pupil Book 1B
Pupil Worksheets 1 (SDMs)
Teacher's Notes 1

Level Two   Pupil Book 2
Pupil Worksheets 2 (SDMs)
Teacher's Notes 2

Level Three Pupil Book 3
Pupil Worksheets 3 (SDMs)
Teacher's Notes 3

Level four Pupil Book 4
Pupil Worksheets 4 (SDMs)
Teacher's Notes 4

In addition, Edith Biggs has written a *Teacher's Guide* which provides the mathematical background and guidance for the overall use of *Macmillan Junior Mathematics*.

The aims

The Cockroft report recommends that: 'Mathematics teaching at all levels should include opportunities for

- exposition by the teacher;
- discussion between teacher and pupils and between the pupils themselves;
- appropriate practical work;
- consolidation and practice of fundamental skills and routines;
- problem solving, including the application of mathematics to everyday situations;
- investigational work.'

Mathematics Counts, HMSO, 1982

All these necessary aspects of good teaching are included in *Macmillan Junior Mathematics* so that the children should:

1. enjoy mathematics,
2. understand not only the concepts, but also the processes of written calculations,
3. become confident in their own ability to understand what they are doing and to solve the problems they meet,
4. know and can use the mathematical vocabulary they require for different concepts,
5. become aware of the importance of pattern in number and shape.

The structure and content

Macmillan Junior Mathematics covers the same eight aspects of Mathematics as the Infant/First School material. These aspects comprise Number and Money (combined); Length; Volume and capacity; Time; Mass and weighing; Area; Shape. They are ordered in each of the pupil books according to conceptual and developmental difficulty.

Work on each aspect within the pupil book is preceded by some introductory pages which serve as a link between one year of the series and the next. There is a comparable link between Year 1 of Macmillan Junior Mathematics and the fourth level of Macmillan Mathematics for the Infant/First School. The introductory pages also enable teachers to find out whether the children are ready for the new work. These pages and the checkpoints at the end of each aspect are designed to help teachers to assess the development of the children's understanding and skills throughout the four-year course.

There are opportunities for practice throughout the books. In addition, the spirit duplicating master worksheets which accompany each level provide further practice, consolidation and, in some cases, extension material. These have been keyed to the text so that they can be used at suitable points during the year.

In the pupils' text, a variety of activities has been introduced to help children to acquire concepts and to use them with understanding. The language of the text has been carefully structured to build up a command of mathematical language patterns. New vocabulary is listed in the teacher's notes.

Much of the work in the series is practical: the children are expected to learn by experiment and discussion. Some equipment and materials are therefore needed, and these are clearly set out in the teacher's notes. Care has been taken to ensure that materials are of a kind readily available, either in schools or at home. Careful organisation of the necessary materials is essential for this way of working.

The teacher's notes which accompany each level are designed to give teachers a thorough understanding of the mathematics the children are learning, and to help them make the most of the series. There are suggestions for extension work, both for slow learners and for the more able children, and ideas for extra revision when the children need to return to a subject again and again. Though the material is complete in itself, teachers can develop it further where necessary, using it as a springboard for their own ideas.

Organisation and methods

The Cockroft report on mathematics emphasised how important it is, at all stages of education, for children to use materials for the learning of mathematics and to discuss what they are doing, not only with their teacher but also with their peers. Both needs arise because mathematics is based on solving problems by the use of the imagination and the interchange of ideas.

These objectives are most easily attained by working with the children in groups when they are actively engaged in acquiring concepts or solving problems. Some children are already accustomed to working in this way, mainly in other aspects of the curriculum. Children who are accustomed to being taught as a class for nearly all of the time will need to be introduced gradually to the responsibilities which group work entails.

Many teachers may not have had previous experience of organising their class in groups. Few of us, if any, learned mathematics ourselves by means of structured activities and investigations – with or without material. Moreover, most of us remember mathematics as a mainly silent lesson. For teachers, too, the change must be gradual if it is to be lasting. Of course the pupils will not always work in groups; exposition by the teacher and practice by the children to consolidate skills are also included in *Macmillan Junior Mathematics*.

One way of achieving the change to group work is for the teacher to concentrate on one group each day, observing individual responses, asking questions and stimulating discussion, while at the same time she provides the remainder of the children with activities which are within their capabilities (making answers available if the children are practising computation).

There is one major prerequisite of successful classroom organisation, whether the children are taught in groups or as a whole class: the preparation of the materials required. All materials should be clearly labelled; teachers need to check that the children know where these are kept and return them to their proper places. They also need to check that the children (who will often work in pairs within a group) know where the material for the next activity is kept.

When *Macmillan Junior Mathematics* has been newly adopted, it would be advantageous for the head and teachers to familiarise themselves in advance with the pupils' books and the teacher's notes. Discussion sessions from time to time when the series is in use will provide opportunities for teachers to recount and compare their experiences and to keep in touch with the way in which the series as a whole is working through the school.

SCOPE AND SEQUENCE CHART

Page	Content	Vocabulary
3, 4	**Number** Introductory spread; odd and even numbers, square numbers, place value, calculations involving the four operations, use of correct language patterns.	
5	**Number** Using a calendar to find multiples of 2.	*multiples*
6	**Number** Addition, subtraction and multiplication of dice scores. Properties of multiples of 10.	
7	**Number** Addition and subtraction of money up to £1.	*possibilities*
8	**Number** Addition of dice scores; using tally marks to record.	
9	**Number** Addition table for numbers 1 to 6. Comparing with dice scores.	*diagonal, vertical, horizontal*
10	**Number** Multiplication of dice scores; finding highest, lowest and impossible scores.	*products*
11	**Number** Multiplication table for numbers 1 to 6. Comparing with dice scores.	
12	**Area** Introductory page. Finding areas using non-standard units; comparing perimeters.	*triangular*
13	**Area** Finding areas using squared paper.	*perimeter*
14	**Area** Irregular areas on centimetre squared paper.	
15	**Area** Areas of successive squares in square centimetres; noticing the pattern.	*square centimetre (sq cm)*
16, 17	**Mass** Introductory spread. Checking understanding of concept and vocabulary; using standard masses (100 g, 500 g, 1 kg)	*kilogram, gram, greater mass, less mass, the same mass as, substance*
18, 19	**Mass** Making and using a simple weighing machine. Comparing masses of small objects.	*extension, contraction*
20	**Mass** Using the machine with standard masses (50 g).	*extension and compression (scales)*
21	**Mass** Using bathroom scales to find masses.	*compression scales*
22, 23	**Number** Making triangular numbers. Application of triangular numbers.	*triangular number, sequence*
24	**Number** Money, using the four operations.	*construction*

vi

Page	Content	Vocabulary
25	**Number** Making 3-digit numbers with dice; arranging in order; finding highest/lowest.	
26	**Number** Making 3-digit numbers with cards; arranging in order.	
27	**Number** Making 2-digit numbers with cards. Finding highest/lowest totals.	
28	**Number** Fractions. Addition and subtraction of halves and quarters.	
29	**Number** Fractions. More work with halves and quarters.	
30, 31	**Number** Introducing and using thirds. Finding halves and quarters; application with money.	*one-third, thirds*
32, 33	**Shape** Introductory spread. Checking understanding of vocabulary associated with 3D shapes; making net of open cube; angles and rigid frames; mirror and rotational patterns.	*cuboid, cylinder, cone, rigid, sphere, net, face, edge, corner, angle, right-angle, horizontal, vertical, hollow*
34	**Shape** Finding and making patterns with mirror symmetry.	*mirror symmetry, mirror line (axis), fabric*
35	**Shape** Recognising mirror symmetry.	*mirror image*
36, 37	**Shape** Making regular pentagons and 5-pointed stars.	*diagonal, pentagon, 5-pointed star*
38, 39	**Shape** Making nets of 3D shapes.	*hexagon, prism*
40	**Length** Introductory page. Checking knowledge of units of length and ability to use these when measuring; the relationship between successive units of length.	*centimetre, decimetre, metre*
41	**Length** Using centimetres and metres.	
42	**Length** Measuring and arranging long jumps in order. Finding differences.	
43	**Length** Introducing concept of average length without using vocabulary.	
44, 45	**Time** Introductory spread. Checking knowledge of months of year, days of week, calendars, and telling and recording time in quarter hours.	*templates*
46, 47	**Time** Reading the time at 5-minute intervals.	*overlap*
48, 49	**Number** Fractions. Addition and subtraction of simple fractions.	
50, 51	**Number** Subtraction. The 'diffy' game with 1- and 2-digit numbers.	

Page	Content	Vocabulary
52	**Number** Multiples of 3,6,9. Making a table. Looking for patterns.	
53	**Number** Table of multiples of 9. Finding sum of the digits.	
54, 55	**Volume and capacity** Introductory spread. Halving a litre of water; finding water with same volume as a large stone; finding pile of pebbles with same volume as the stone.	*litre*
56, 57	**Volume and capacity** Finding capacity in litres of buckets and watering cans. Finding volume of water used on the school garden.	*square metre*
58, 59	**Volume and capacity** The millilitre. Working with containers of capacities 5 ml to 500 ml. Estimating capacities of domestic containers.	*millilitre (ml), graduated, graduations, successive*
60	**Area** Areas of squares and rectangles in square centimetres.	
61	**Area** Finding dimensions, number patterns and areas of rectangles with same perimeter.	*increase, decrease*
62, 63	**Area** Arranging rectangles with same perimeter in mathematical pattern.	
64	**Area** Making table showing width, length and area of given rectangles.	
65	**Number** Multiplication. Drawing on squared paper; Expanded form. Practice and problems.	
66	**Number** Division of numbers from 11 to 66 by single-digit numbers. Multiplication check.	
67	**Number** Division. Finding remainders using dice scores.	
68, 69	**Number** Building sequences of squares. Describing patterns.	*enlarging, layer*
70	**Number** Money problems requiring use of the four operations.	
71	**Number** Division of money using repeated subtraction.	
72	**Number** Division problems and practice.	
73, 74	**Shape** Investigating shapes with rotational symmetry.	*rotational symmetry, centre of rotation, angle of turn*
75	**Shape** Using two parallelograms to make shapes with rotational and mirror symmetry. Investigating perimeters.	

Page	Content	Vocabulary
76	**Shape** Finding axes of mirror symmetry. Comparing with rotational symmetry.	axis, axes
77	**Shape** Making series of paper squares by repeated folding.	reducing
78, 79	**Shape** Enlarging 2D shapes and finding area and perimeter patterns.	dimension
80	**Length** Measuring and comparing perimeters.	exchange roles
81	**Length** Introducing the ratio of two lengths.	ratio (comparison by division)
82	**Length** Ratio of perimeter (circumference) and diameter of circles.	circumference, diameter, ratio, circular
83	**Length** Measuring in decimetres and centimetres. Arranging lengths in order.	
84	**Length** Using lengths for comparison, applying the four operations.	
85, 86	**Length** Revision.	circumference, diameter
87	**Number** Addition and subtraction in number puzzles.	
88, 89	**Number** Finding relationship between the edge and perimeter of squares. Showing this relationship graphically.	vertical
90, 91	**Number** Introducing decimals using the decimetre.	decimal
92	**Time** Referring to am and pm, midday and midnight.	am (ante meridian), pm (post meridian), midday, noon, midnight
93	**Time** Drawing shadows at different times of day.	
94	**Time** Introducing the seasons through birthday months.	seasons
95	**Time** Finding the duration of television programmes.	
96, 97	**Volume and capacity** Making (a) irregular shapes, (b) cuboids, of same volume using interlocking cubes. Finding 'skin' area of shapes.	dimensions
98, 99	**Volume and capacity** Working with millilitres.	graduated, graduation
100	**Volume and capacity** Revision.	prescribe
101, 102	**Number** Finding and recording body measurements in dm and cm. Arranging in order; recording as decimals of dm. Finding differences between body measurements.	

ix

Page	Content	Vocabulary
103	**Number** Adding and subtracting decimal lengths.	
104	**Number** Doubling decimal lengths.	
105	**Number** Addition, subtraction, multiplication and division practice.	
106	**Mass** Finding the point of balance of different objects.	*point of balance*
107	**Mass** Finding the point of balance of a broom.	
108, 109	**Mass** Comparing masses of flour and sugar. Cooking, and weighing ingredients.	
110	**Mass** Experimenting with point of balance.	
111	**Mass** Revision.	*net mass, compression*
112, 113	**Shape** Using a template to make patterns with (a) rotational symmetry and (b) mirror symmetry.	*template*
114, 115	**Shape** Revision.	*octagon, parallelogram, right-angled triangle, isosceles triangle, centre of rotation*
116, 117	**Number** Games; building a cube, breaking a cube, addition of decimals.	
118	**Number** Multiplying and dividing by 1. Multiplying by zero, adding zero, subtracting zero.	
119	**Number** Reversing 2-digit numbers and looking for patterns.	
120, 121	**Number** Revision.	
122, 123	**Area** Revision.	
124	**Time** Duration of time spanning midnight.	
125	**Time** Introducing and using the 24-hour clock for times after midday.	*24-hour clock*
126, 127	**Time** Revision.	

Number

Pages 3 and 4 Introducing number

Content
Checking that the children can (a) recognise odd and even numbers, square numbers; (b) understand place value; (c) carry out, with understanding, calculations using the four operations; (d) use the correct language patterns.

Equipment
Those children who have difficulty with any of these problems should be provided with appropriate material, such as ten-sticks and units, and given suitable activities.

Notes
1. The introductory pages which accompany each unit in this book are intended as revision of the previous year's work. If the children have difficulty with any of the questions, they should be referred back to the relevant pages in Books 1A or 1B.

Q4   20, 16

Q6   (a) (i) 34   (ii) 102   (iii) 64   (iv) 112

Q7   (a) 40p   (b) 27p   (c) 10p   (d) 44p

Q8   (a) 10   (b) 16   (c) $\frac{3}{4}$ (d) 24

Q9   (a) 3   (b) 0   (c) 6   (d) $\frac{1}{2}$

Q10   29, 37, 45, 53, 61.
The pattern is 5, 4, 3, 2, 1, 9, 8, 7. It continues to 1 and then starts with 9 again. Check that the children are not counting in ones when adding 8.

Q11   (a) 87   (b) 42   (c) 86   (d) 42
      (e) 55   (f) 26   (g) 81   (h) 16

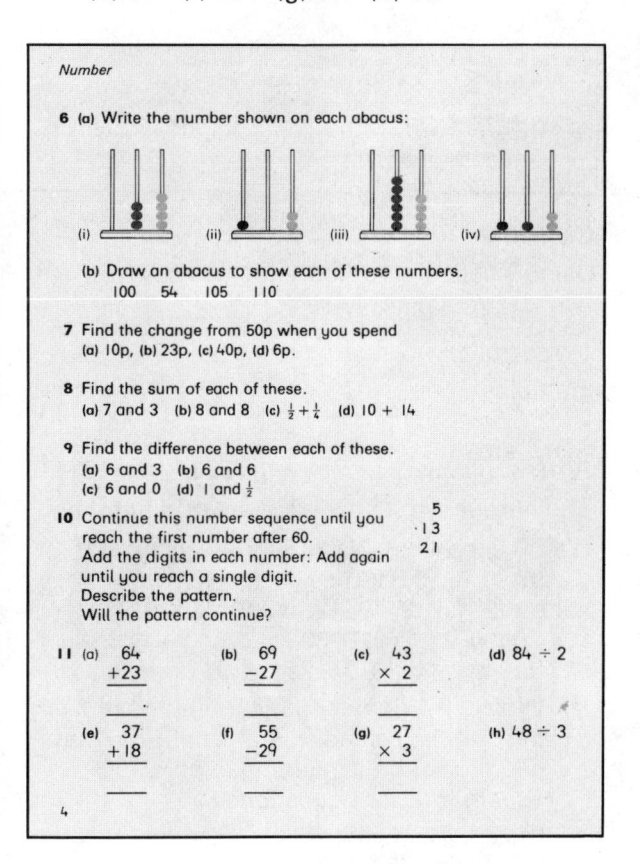

Number

Introducing number

1 Put these into two sets (odds and evens).
   17   52   64   101   110   111   125   100

2 Make (i) the largest number and (ii) the smallest number you can with these digits.
   (a) 5, 8   (b) 0, 9   (c) 6, 7, 2   (d) 8, 0, 1

3 Find the difference between 31 and 13.
Use a number line to show how you did this.
Check by using the shopkeeper's method.

4 How many unit squares are there in this square frame?
How many unit squares could you put in the middle?

5 Make up two stories to fit this division.
   24 ÷ 4

Number

6 (a) Write the number shown on each abacus:
   (i)   (ii)   (iii)   (iv)

(b) Draw an abacus to show each of these numbers.
   100   54   105   110

7 Find the change from 50p when you spend
   (a) 10p, (b) 23p, (c) 40p, (d) 6p.

8 Find the sum of each of these.
   (a) 7 and 3   (b) 8 and 8   (c) $\frac{1}{2} + \frac{1}{4}$ (d) 10 + 14

9 Find the difference between each of these.
   (a) 6 and 3   (b) 6 and 6
   (c) 6 and 0   (d) 1 and $\frac{1}{2}$

10 Continue this number sequence until you reach the first number after 60.
Add the digits in each number: Add again until you reach a single digit.
Describe the pattern.
Will the pattern continue?
   5, 13, 21

11 (a) 64 + 23   (b) 69 − 27   (c) 43 × 2   (d) 84 ÷ 2
    (e) 37 + 18   (f) 55 − 29   (g) 27 × 3   (h) 48 ÷ 3

Page 5 Calendar patterns

Calendar patterns

1 Here is a calendar for December. Some of the numbers have been shaded. What patterns do they make? Write down the first 10 numbers that are shaded in. These are called **multiples of 2**. What do they remind you of? What are the numbers that are not multiples of 2 called?

December 1985

Sun	Mon	Tues	Wed	Thurs	Fri	Sat
1	2	3	4	5	6	7
8	9	10	11	12	13	14
15	16	17	18	19	20	21
22	23	24	25	26	27	28
29	30	31				

2 Write down the multiples of 2:
(a) between 21 and 31,
(b) between 5 and 15,
(c) fewer than 21,
(d) in the twenties,
(e) that end in 4 or 8 are fewer than 30,
(f) between 31 and 41,
(g) between 71 and 81,
(h) more than 43 but fewer than 65,
(i) fewer than 100 but more than 90.

Content
Using a calendar to find multiples of 2.

Vocabulary
multiples

Notes
The numbers not shaded in are odd numbers.

Q2 (a) 22, 24, 26, 28, 30.
   (b) 6, 8, 10, 12, 14.
   (c) 2, 4, 6, 8, 10, 12, 14, 16, 18, 20.
   (d) 20; 22, 24, 26, 28.
   (e) 4, 8, 14, 18, 24, 28.
   (Note: (f) – (i) extend the multiples of 2 beyond the calendar. Some children may need to continue shading in on a 100-square for these questions.)
   (f) 32, 34, 36, 38, 40.
   (g) 72, 74, 76, 78, 80.
   (h) 44, 46, 48, 50, 52, 54, 56, 58, 60, 62, 64.
   (i) 92, 94, 96, 98.

Extend this work by looking at other multiples.

Page 6 Ten times as much

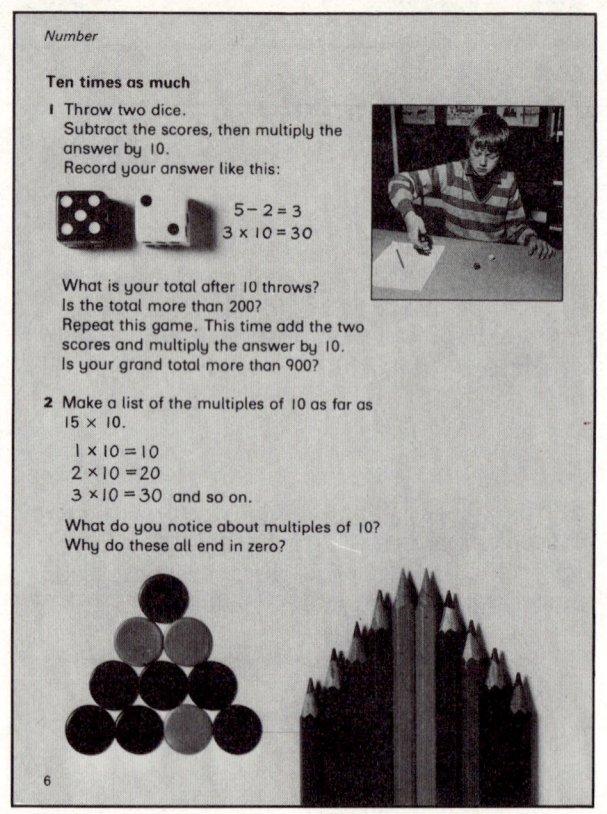

Ten times as much

1 Throw two dice. Subtract the scores, then multiply the answer by 10. Record your answer like this:

$5 - 2 = 3$
$3 \times 10 = 30$

What is your total after 10 throws? Is the total more than 200? Repeat this game. This time add the two scores and multiply the answer by 10. Is your grand total more than 900?

2 Make a list of the multiples of 10 as far as 15×10.

$1 \times 10 = 10$
$2 \times 10 = 20$
$3 \times 10 = 30$ and so on.

What do you notice about multiples of 10? Why do these all end in zero?

Content
Throwing two dice and subtracting or adding the scores; multiplying the result by 10. Properties of multiples of 10.

Equipment
dice

Notes
Q1 Ask what the highest score would be. For subtracting it is 500. For addition it is 1200.

Q2 All multiples of 10 end in zero because there are no units. They are all tens. Some children may need ten-sticks to help them.

Page 7 At the fair

At the fair

1. If you go to the fair and try everything in turn, how much will you spend?

Roundabout	25p
Swings	10p
Helter-skelter	15p
Dodgems	30p
Big Wheel	35p
Ghost Train	20p
Throw a hoop	15p

2. You have £1 to spend. You can choose what to do: How would you spend £1?
   Make a list of the things you choose and the total cost.
   How much change would you have?
   Make another list of things you could do.
   How much is left this time?

3. Can you make a choice so that you spend exactly £1?
   Write down this choice.

4. Peter needs £1 in change.
   How many of each of the following coins would he get?
   (a) 10p (b) 50p (c) 20p (d) 5p
   (e) mixed 10p and 20p
   Write all the possibilities for (e).

Content
Addition and subtraction of money up to £1.

Vocabulary
possibilities

Equipment
coins (5p to 50p)

Notes

1. Some children will need to use money to count out change.

Q1 £1·50

Q4 (e) 10 × 10p and 0 × 20p;
8 × 10p and 1 × 20p; 6 × 10p and 2 × 20p;
4 × 10p and 3 × 20p; 2 × 10p and 4 × 20p;
0 × 10p and 5 × 20p

2. *Extend* this (i) by using larger amounts of money, (ii) by using 5p and 10p coins as change.

Worksheet 1 provides extra practice, in puzzle and table form, of addition, subtraction and multiplication.

Answers

1

3	+	7	+	4	=14
+		+		+	
8	+	2	+	6	=16
+		+		+	
4	+	3	+	9	=16
=15		=12		=19	

8	×	2	−	4	=12
×		×		×	
3	×	2	+	5	=11
−		+		−	
9	×	2	−	8	=10
=16		=6		=12	

2

+	7p	9p	11p	13p	15p	17p	19p	8p	12p	14p	16p	18p
3p	10p	12p	14p	16p	18p	20p	22p	11p	15p	17p	19p	21p
5p	12p	14p	16p	18p	20p	22p	24p	13p	17p	19p	21p	23p
7p	14p	16p	18p	20p	22p	24p	26p	15p	19p	21p	23p	25p
8p	15p	17p	19p	21p	23p	25p	27p	16p	20p	22p	24p	26p
9p	16p	18p	20p	22p	24p	26p	28p	17p	21p	23p	25p	27p

×	1	2	3	4	5	6	7	8	9	10
2p	2p	4p	6p	8p	10p	12p	14p	16p	18p	20p
3p	3p	6p	9p	12p	15p	18p	21p	24p	27p	30p
4p	4p	8p	12p	16p	20p	24p	28p	32p	36p	40p
5p	5p	10p	15p	20p	25p	30p	35p	40p	45p	50p
10p	10p	20p	30p	40p	50p	60p	70p	80p	90p	100p

Page 8 Make a gate

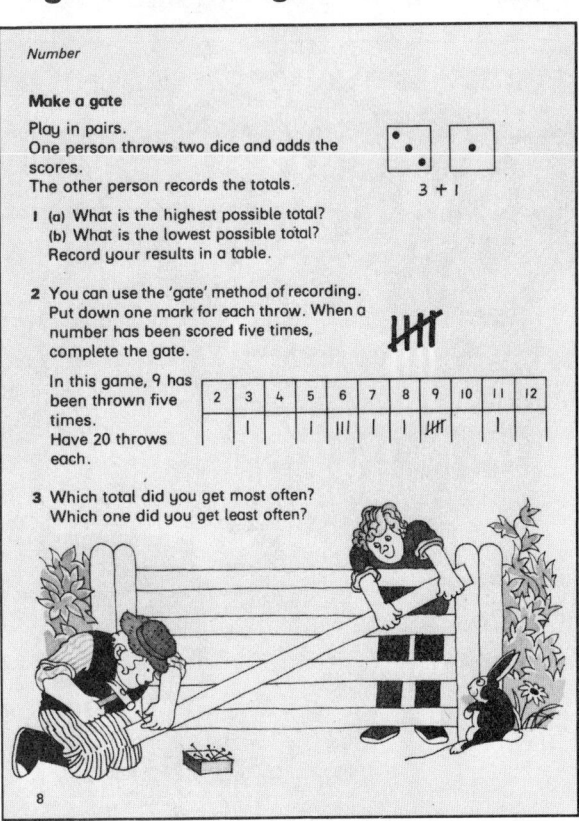

Make a gate

Play in pairs.
One person throws two dice and adds the scores.
The other person records the totals.

3 + 1

1. (a) What is the highest possible total?
   (b) What is the lowest possible total?
   Record your results in a table.

2. You can use the 'gate' method of recording. Put down one mark for each throw. When a number has been scored five times, complete the gate.

In this game, 9 has been thrown five times.
Have 20 throws each.

2	3	4	5	6	7	8	9	10	11	12
	I		III		I		ℍ	I		

3. Which total did you get most often?
   Which one did you get least often?

Content

Introducing tally marks as a method of recording the addition of scores after throwing two dice.

Equipment

dice

Notes

1. Check that the children see the purpose of using the gate method. Let them record by another method first. The gate method is quicker when finding totals, and encourages children to learn the number pattern for the multiples of 5.

Q1 The highest possible total is 12, the lowest is 2.

Q3 Numbers that should appear most frequently are 6, 7, 8. Least frequent scores are 2 and 12.

2. *Extend* by collecting more results. Two pairs of children could combine their results and discuss these.

Page 9 An addition table

An addition table

1 Make an addition table for the numbers 1 to 6.
Start with a row of numbers 1 to 6 along the bottom.
Add 1 to the bottom row to make the first row in the table.
Add 2 to the bottom row to make the second row.
Carry on like this until the table is complete.

Number

6						
5						
4						
3	4	5				
2	3	4	5	6	7	
1	2	3	4	5	6	7
+	1	2	3	4	5	6

2 Which number occurs most often in the table?
Which numbers occur least often?
Are these the numbers that you scored most often and least often with the dice?
Which totals occur the same number of times in the table?

3 What is the same about this table and finding the sum of two numbers with dice?

Q. Which snakes are best at sums?
A. Adders.

4 Now collect results from another group and add their totals to yours.
Which number did both groups together score most often?

5 Put a ring round all the sixes in the table.
What do you know about all these sixes?

Content

Making an addition table for the numbers 1 to 6. Comparing this table with the results from the dice experiment.

Vocabulary

diagonal, vertical, horizontal

Notes

Q1 Some children find it helpful if the numbers outside the table are in a different colour so that they can easily see which numbers they are adding together.

Q2 Ask the children to comment on any patterns or arrangements of numbers that they see before drawing their attention to the numbers that occur most and least often. 7 usually occurs most often, while 2 and 12 occur least often.

Q3 The dice experiment and the table resemble each other in that both use the numbers 1 to 6. The table includes all the sums of pairs of numbers from 1 to 6, but in the dice experiment some may be omitted.

Q4 By combining other results it is possible for the class to see that their experimental results resemble those in the table.

Q5 All the totals of 6 are in a diagonal line.

Extend for some children by considering how near the class results are to those in the table, eg in the table, 7 occurs $\frac{1}{6}$ of the time. A calculator could be used to see how near the class results are to this fraction.

Page 10 Multiplying with dice

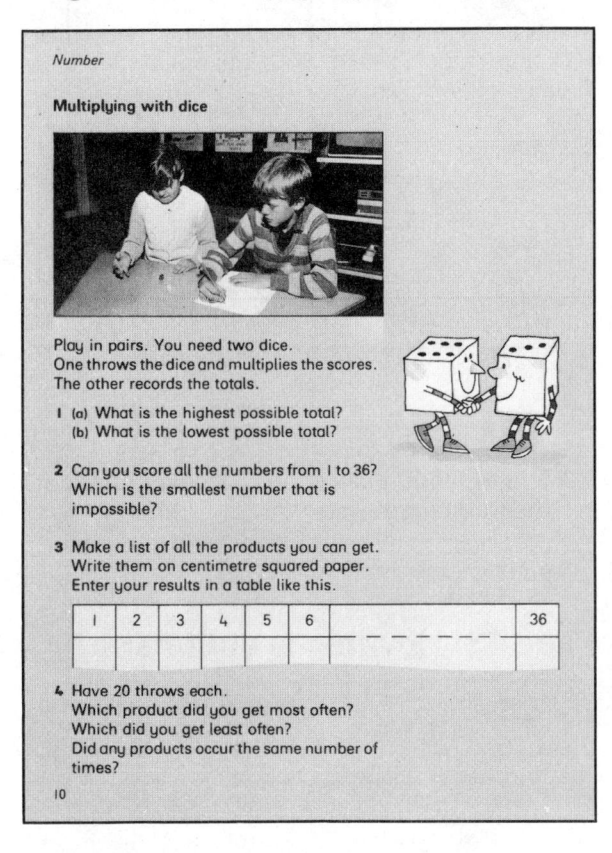

Number
Multiplying with dice

Play in pairs. You need two dice.
One throws the dice and multiplies the scores.
The other records the totals.

1. (a) What is the highest possible total?
   (b) What is the lowest possible total?

2. Can you score all the numbers from 1 to 36? Which is the smallest number that is impossible?

3. Make a list of all the products you can get. Write them on centimetre squared paper. Enter your results in a table like this.

1	2	3	4	5	6	—	—	—	36

4. Have 20 throws each.
   Which product did you get most often?
   Which did you get least often?
   Did any products occur the same number of times?

Content
Multiplying scores on two dice; finding the highest and lowest scores, as well as impossible scores in the range 1 to 36.

Vocabulary
products

Equipment
dice

Notes
1. Watch how individual children approach the task of finding impossible scores.

   Q2 The first impossible score is 7. Others are 11, 13, 14, 17 19, 21, 22, 23, 26, 27, 28, 29, 31, 32, 33, 34, 35.

2. *Extend* this work with the more able by collecting many more results and considering which score should occur most often, and why. From 20 results it is impossible to predict which of the scores will occur most or least often.

Page 11 A multiplication table

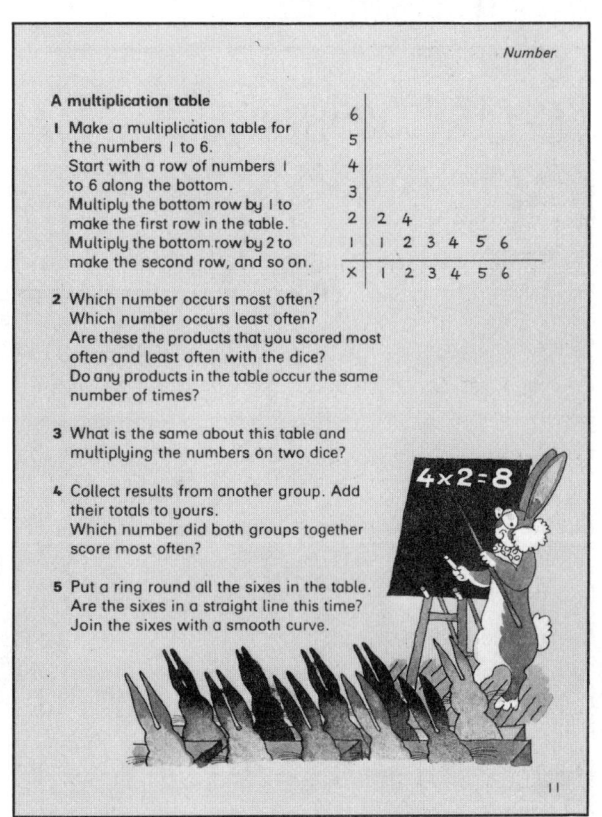

Number
A multiplication table

1. Make a multiplication table for the numbers 1 to 6.
   Start with a row of numbers 1 to 6 along the bottom.
   Multiply the bottom row by 1 to make the first row in the table.
   Multiply the bottom row by 2 to make the second row, and so on.

6						
5						
4						
3						
2	2	4				
1	1	2	3	4	5	6
×	1	2	3	4	5	6

2. Which number occurs most often?
   Which number occurs least often?
   Are these the products that you scored most often and least often with the dice?
   Do any products in the table occur the same number of times?

3. What is the same about this table and multiplying the numbers on two dice?

4. Collect results from another group. Add their totals to yours.
   Which number did both groups together score most often?

5. Put a ring round all the sixes in the table.
   Are the sixes in a straight line this time?
   Join the sixes with a smooth curve.

Content
Making a multiplication table for the numbers 1 to 6, and comparing this with the results obtained by throwing two dice and multiplying the scores.

Notes
Q1 Ask the children whether they can see any patterns. The square numbers occur in a diagonal from bottom left to top right.

Q2 The numbers 6 and 12 occur most often. The numbers 1, 9, 16, 25, 36 only occur once; some children should notice that these are square numbers less than 40 with 4 missing. Ask why 4 is missing from the set of numbers that occur only once. Why does 4 occur more than once?

Q3 The dice experiment and the table resemble each other in that both use the numbers 1 to 6. The table includes all the products of pairs of numbers from 1 to 6, but in the dice experiment some may be omitted.

Q5 When the 6s are ringed they form a curve.

5

Area

Page 12 Introducing area

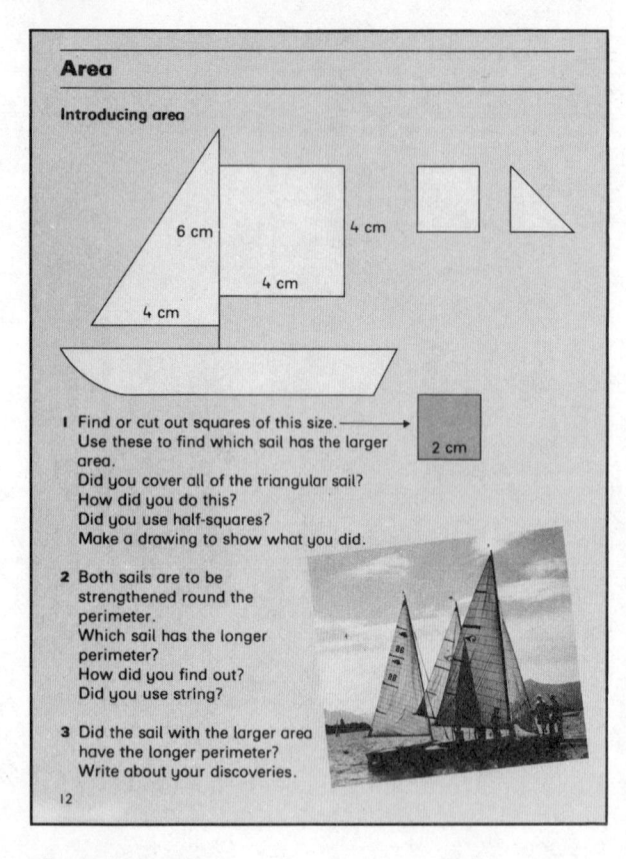

Area
Introducing area

1 Find or cut out squares of this size.
Use these to find which sail has the larger area.
Did you cover all of the triangular sail?
How did you do this?
Did you use half-squares?
Make a drawing to show what you did.

2 Both sails are to be strengthened round the perimeter.
Which sail has the longer perimeter?
How did you find out?
Did you use string?

3 Did the sail with the larger area have the longer perimeter?
Write about your discoveries.

Content
Finding areas using non-standard units (squares and half-squares); comparing perimeters.

Vocabulary
triangular

Equipment
plastic or thick paper squares (2 cm edge), thin string (not nylon)

Notes

Q1 The area of the square is 4 square units and the area of the triangle is 3 square units (the square units will not fit in exactly). The children can obtain an approximate answer by using half-squares.

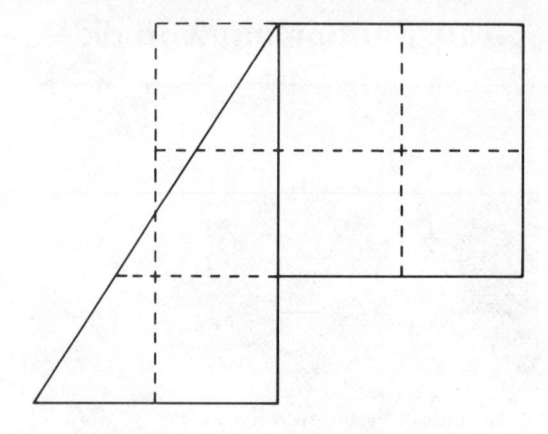

Q2 The children can compare the perimeters of the sails by using string.

Q3 The triangular sail has the smaller area but the longer perimeter. Ask the children to comment on the area and perimeter of the square sail.

Page 13 How big is your hand?

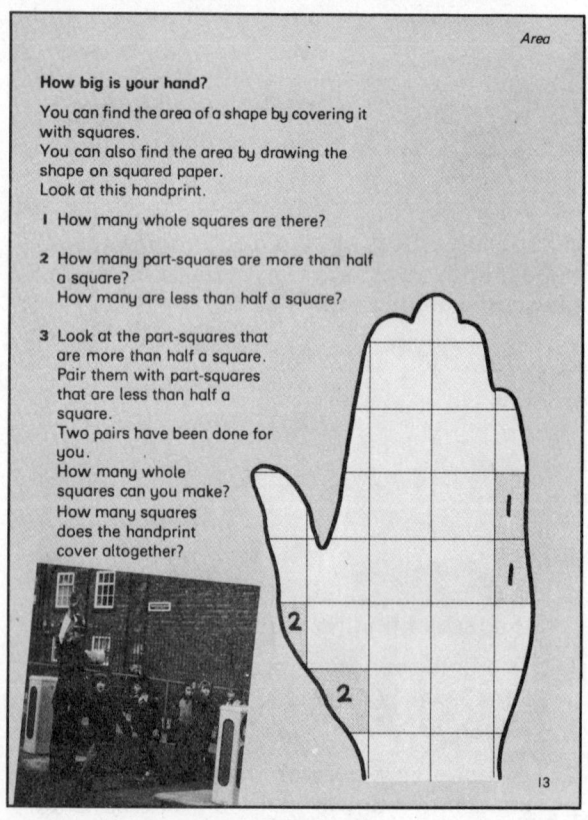

How big is your hand?

You can find the area of a shape by covering it with squares.
You can also find the area by drawing the shape on squared paper.
Look at this handprint.

1 How many whole squares are there?

2 How many part-squares are more than half a square?
How many are less than half a square?

3 Look at the part-squares that are more than half a square.
Pair them with part-squares that are less than half a square.
Two pairs have been done for you.
How many whole squares can you make?
How many squares does the handprint cover altogether?

Content
Finding areas using squared paper, and estimating the area of part-squares.

Vocabulary
perimeter

Equipment
2-centimetre squared paper

Notes
1. Precede this page by finding the area of the outline of the back of the smallest child in square decimetres. Each child in the class can cut out one or two square decimetres from squared paper. These are used to cover the area inside the outline. Ask the children what they should do about the part-squares. If they do not respond by folding a square decimetre in half and fitting this in a space, ask if they could fit in half-squares. Ask how they will count the half-squares (by pairing).

2. Work with a group, as some children will need help in pairing part-squares. First suggest they pair the squares they think are half-squares. Then they can pair squares that are more and less than half a square.

3. *Extend* by letting the children find the areas of other non-rectangular shapes such as circles and hexagons.

Page 14 Porky the Pig

Content
Finding an irregular area using centimetre squared paper.

Equipment
centimetre squared paper, coloured pencils or paint

Notes
1. The children can draw the shape freehand.

2. If the children have difficulty, suggest they count the whole squares first. They need to mark the squares as they count them and keep a record. Give help with counting the part-squares if necessary — for example, ask 'How many half-squares are there?' 'How many squares are more than half, less than half?' etc.

3. Ask the children if they can find the area as an exact number of squares. Discuss approximation.

4. Make a display on the classroom wall. The animal shapes could be labelled with their areas in square centimetres and coloured.

Page 15 Growing squares

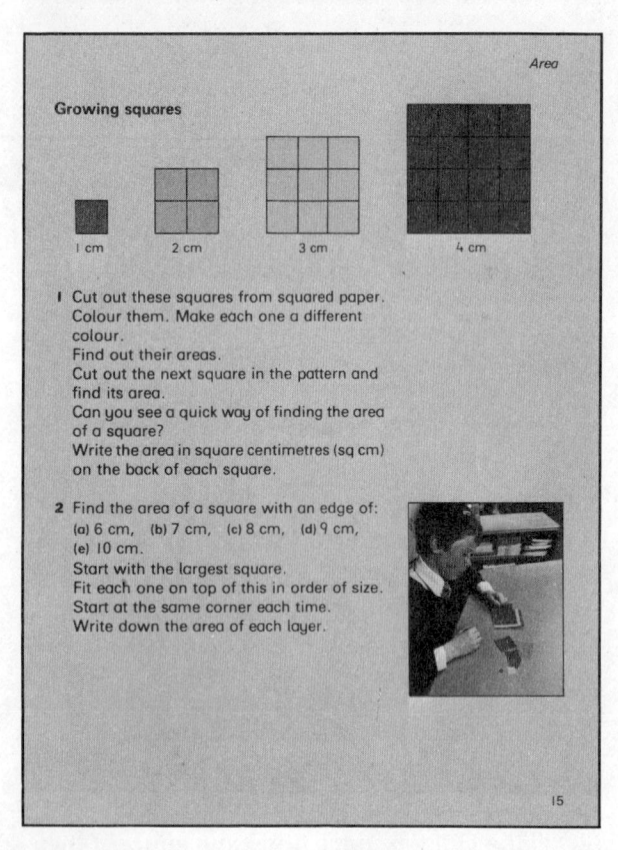

Content
Finding the areas of successive squares in square centimetres, and noticing the pattern they make.

Vocabulary
square centimetre (sq cm)

Equipment
centimetre squared paper, scissors, coloured pencils

Notes
1. Check that the children are not counting every unit square but are finding the areas by multiplication.
2. Ask the children if they recognise this sequence of numbers (square numbers).
3. The layers are 1, 3, 5, etc. Ask the children what they know about these numbers. See if they can extend the sequence of odd numbers.
4. Let them make a display of the patterns.
5. *Extend* by asking if the children can make a different pattern by placing squares on top of the largest square, eg all 'odd' squares or 'even' squares on top of one another.

Worksheet 2 can be used here to provide extra practice in calculating areas using squared grids.

Answers
2 15, $4\frac{1}{2}$, 6, 15 and 16 square centimetres.

Mass

Introduction

Reasons why the word 'mass' should be used when the standard units are kilograms (kg) and grams (g).

In the past, because distinct and different units were not used when measuring mass and measuring weight, these two concepts were often confused. We referred to 'weighing' and 'weight' when we were using units of mass (pounds). The two concepts are entirely different however, although it is not easy to explain the differences to young children.

Kilograms and grams are units of mass, and in this book we shall therefore use the word 'mass' when working in these units.

If we want to give a rigorous definition of 'mass', we have to use the concept of acceleration. Because this concept is not easy, such a definition is normally not introduced until the secondary stage. At the primary level, the mass of an object can be described as the amount of material or stuff in it, measured in kilograms and grams. (An object's volume is the amount of space it occupies, measured in cubic metres, cubic centimetres, etc.)

The mass of an object does not change when its position changes. Astronauts have the same mass on the Moon as they have on the Earth.

If we are balancing (using balance scales) an object in one pan against standard masses (eg kilograms or grams) in the other pan, this process can be referred to as 'weighing', but we should use the statement 'The mass of this object is 1 kilogram' when describing the result.

Weight is a force. Forces always occur in pairs, acting in opposite directions, and they can be felt by pushing or pulling (eg in a tug of war). Weight is the strength of the force of gravity, which operates from the centre of the Earth, other planets or the Moon. The weight of an object can change as the object is moved from one position to another (eg up a mountain, down a coalmine).

From space flight, many children realise that the Earth's pull grows weaker the farther the capsule is from the Earth's centre (inverse relation). On the way to the Moon there is one point at which the capsule and its contents are 'weightless'. This is the point at which the pull of the Moon on the capsule is equal (and opposite) to the pull of the Earth. Elsewhere, the apparent weightlessness of astronauts within the capsule is caused by the motion of the capsule.

The unit of force (weight) is the newton. To experience a force of 1 newton, hold an apple of mass 100 grams in the palm of your hand. The pressure you experience on your hand is of magnitude 1 newton.

Footnote See *Using the environment: 2. Investigations, Part I* by Margaret Collis (Macdonald Educational, 1974) pp 35–51.

Pages 16 and 17 Introducing mass

Content

Checking that the children (a) understand the concept and vocabulary of mass; (b) can use standard masses (100 g, 500 g, 1 kg).

Vocabulary

kilogram, gram, greater mass, less mass, the same mass as, substance

Equipment

large shells or stones or potatoes, balance scales, 500 g masses, objects with mass of about 500 g, 100 g masses, marbles, cotton reels, sheets of paper, strong plastic bags and fasteners, sand, identical plastic containers

Notes

The children should work in pairs for all these activities.

Q1 Ask, 'Which shell has the greatest mass? Which has the least mass? Do any shells have the same mass?' Some children may make many comparisons. Others will develop a strategy. Ask them to talk about what they did, eg 'I balanced the shell I thought had the greatest mass with each of the others in turn. I was right. Then I balanced the other two.'

Q2 When the masses of two objects are compared in the palms of the hands, the wrong conclusions may be drawn. Only if the areas in contact with the hands are the same should a comparison be made. Let

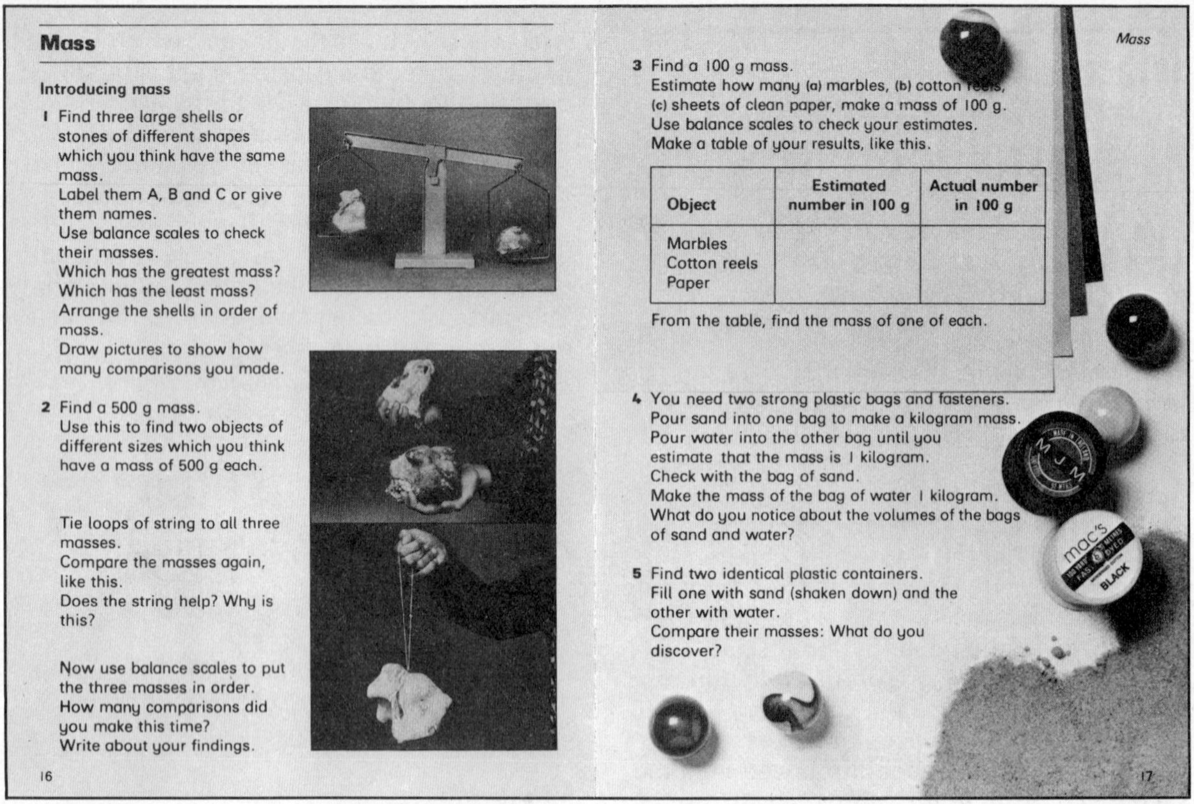

Mass

Introducing mass

1. Find three large shells or stones of different shapes which you think have the same mass.
   Label them A, B and C or give them names.
   Use balance scales to check their masses.
   Which has the greatest mass?
   Which has the least mass?
   Arrange the shells in order of mass.
   Draw pictures to show how many comparisons you made.

2. Find a 500 g mass.
   Use this to find two objects of different sizes which you think have a mass of 500 g each.

   Tie loops of string to all three masses.
   Compare the masses again, like this.
   Does the string help? Why is this?

   Now use balance scales to put the three masses in order.
   How many comparisons did you make this time?
   Write about your findings.

3. Find a 100 g mass.
   Estimate how many (a) marbles, (b) cotton reels, (c) sheets of clean paper, make a mass of 100 g.
   Use balance scales to check your estimates.
   Make a table of your results, like this.

Object	Estimated number in 100 g	Actual number in 100 g
Marbles		
Cotton reels		
Paper		

   From the table, find the mass of one of each.

4. You need two strong plastic bags and fasteners.
   Pour sand into one bag to make a kilogram mass.
   Pour water into the other bag until you estimate that the mass is 1 kilogram.
   Check with the bag of sand.
   Make the mass of the bag of water 1 kilogram.
   What do you notice about the volumes of the bags of sand and water?

5. Find two identical plastic containers.
   Fill one with sand (shaken down) and the other with water.
   Compare their masses: What do you discover?

---

the children experiment by holding a small metal mass in one hand and a large block of polystyrene in the other. However, if the objects are compared, one in each hand on loops of string, a more accurate comparison can be made. (Even so, the children may not find the comparison easy.) Encourage them to make as few comparisons as possible when arranging three masses in order.

Q3 The number of objects should be between 20 and 25. If a calculator is available, the children may use this to find the mass of one object. They will be surprised when they discover the mass of a sheet of paper. Ask them to compare on their hands a flat sheet of paper and a sheet screwed into a ball. Ask them why the masses feel so different.

Q4 The bag of water would have about twice the volume of the bag of sand. Ask the children to explain the difference.

Q5 Ask the children to explain their discoveries. (The mass of sand is greater than the mass of the same volume of water, because sand is a heavier substance than water.)

Pages 18 and 19 Make a weighing machine

Content
Making and using a simple machine for finding the mass of an object.

Vocabulary
extension, contraction

Equipment
yoghurt pots, elastic bands, pencils, marbles, large stones and other objects, rulers or stiff card or boxes (as in pupils' book)

Notes

1. The elastic bands should be from a new packet. Each should be 25–30 cm long and 3 mm wide. Have available objects heavy enough to stretch the bands, eg large stones.
   Discuss with the children how they can show the stretch (extension). They should suggest marking the level of the bottom (or top) of the pot, before and after the objects are added. Marks can be made on stiff card or on a ruler or box held vertically.

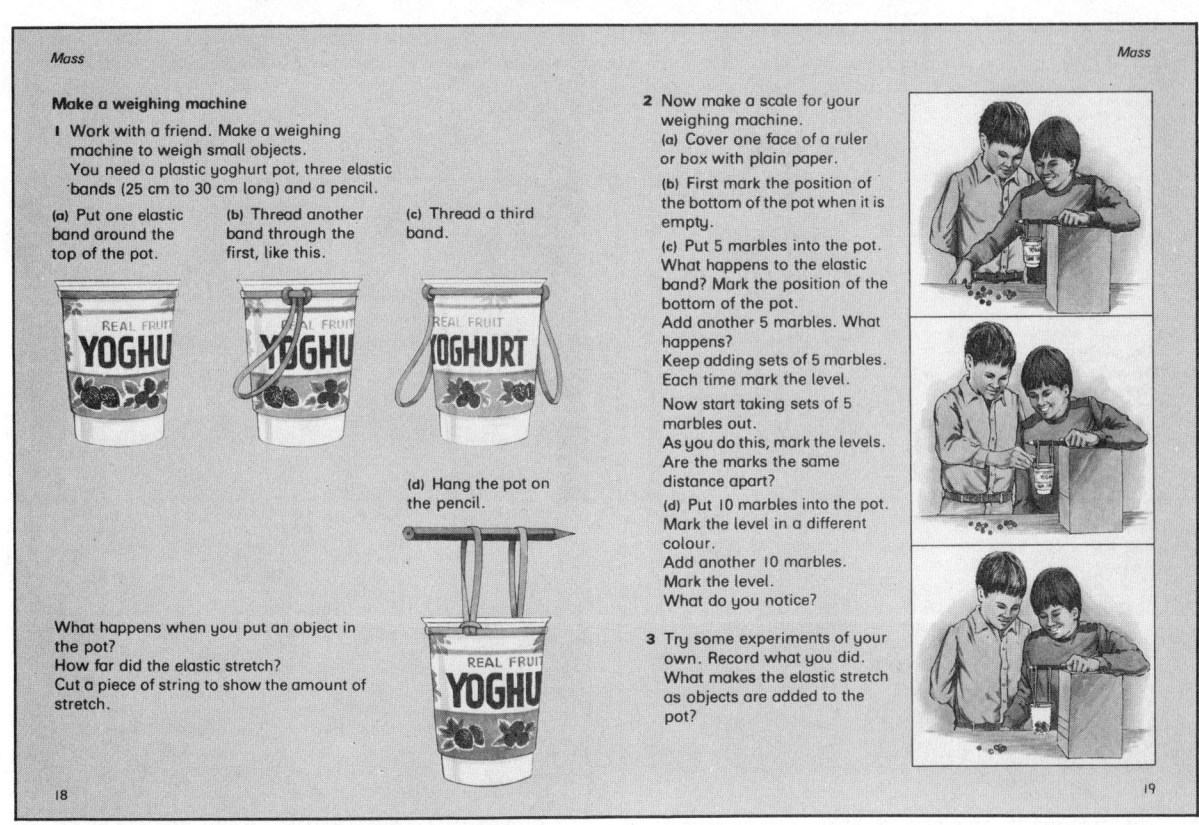

Mass

Make a weighing machine

1. Work with a friend. Make a weighing machine to weigh small objects.
   You need a plastic yoghurt pot, three elastic bands (25 cm to 30 cm long) and a pencil.

   (a) Put one elastic band around the top of the pot.

   (b) Thread another band through the first, like this.

   (c) Thread a third band.

   (d) Hang the pot on the pencil.

   What happens when you put an object in the pot?
   How far did the elastic stretch?
   Cut a piece of string to show the amount of stretch.

2. Now make a scale for your weighing machine.
   (a) Cover one face of a ruler or box with plain paper.
   (b) First mark the position of the bottom of the pot when it is empty.
   (c) Put 5 marbles into the pot. What happens to the elastic band? Mark the position of the bottom of the pot.
   Add another 5 marbles. What happens?
   Keep adding sets of 5 marbles. Each time mark the level.
   Now start taking sets of 5 marbles out.
   As you do this, mark the levels. Are the marks the same distance apart?
   (d) Put 10 marbles into the pot. Mark the level in a different colour.
   Add another 10 marbles. Mark the level.
   What do you notice?

3. Try some experiments of your own. Record what you did. What makes the elastic stretch as objects are added to the pot?

---

2. The pencil holding the yoghurt pot should be supported on the top of a ruler or box. It is easier to mark the level of the bottom of the pot. The children should be at eye-level when marking the scale. After the initial experiment, the children may find it useful to fix squared paper to the scale.

3. When the first five marbles are added, the extension may be different from subsequent extensions (caused by slack in the elastic band). Try the experiment yourself first.

4. Ask the children to show you how much the elastic bands lengthen each time (distance between successive marks).

5. The contraction of the elastic as the marbles are removed may not be the same as the extension. If you use a spring instead of an elastic band, the extension is regular. Ask the children to use a different colour to record the levels as marbles are removed.

6. Encourage the children to use their home-made machines to find objects with the same masses as those shown on their scale.

7. *Extend* by using a light spring (such as those obtainable from motor cycle shops) and asking the children to compare the results.

Q2 Ask the children whether the extension made by ten marbles is twice that made by five marbles.

Page 20 Using your weighing machine

Content

Using the home-made weighing machine with standard masses (50 g).

Vocabulary

extension and compression (scales)

Equipment

home-made weighing machines, stones or plasticine with masses of 50 g, 100 g, 150 g, 200 g, elastic bands, rulers or stiff card or boxes, balance scales, springs or spring scales (extension and compression)

Mass

Using your weighing machine

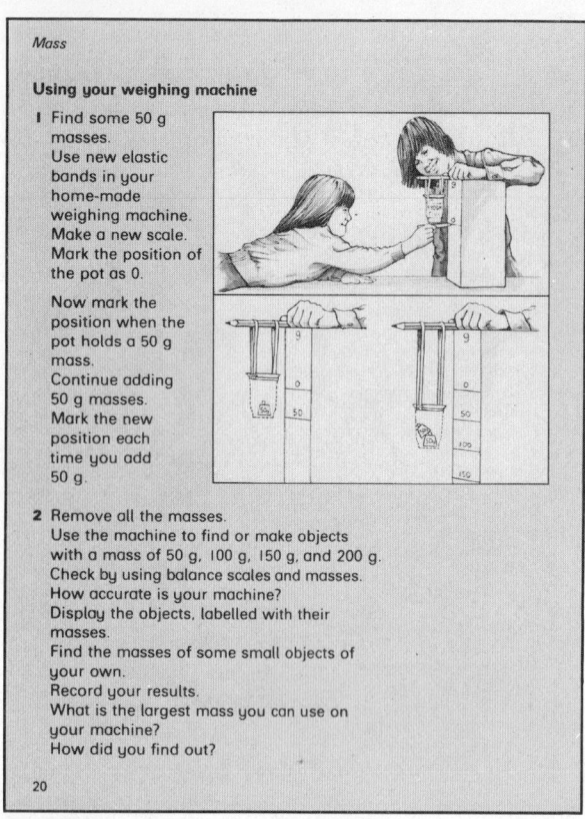

1. Find some 50 g masses.
   Use new elastic bands in your home-made weighing machine.
   Make a new scale.
   Mark the position of the pot as 0.
   Now mark the position when the pot holds a 50 g mass.
   Continue adding 50 g masses.
   Mark the new position each time you add 50 g.

2. Remove all the masses.
   Use the machine to find or make objects with a mass of 50 g, 100 g, 150 g, and 200 g.
   Check by using balance scales and masses.
   How accurate is your machine?
   Display the objects, labelled with their masses.
   Find the masses of some small objects of your own.
   Record your results.
   What is the largest mass you can use on your machine?
   How did you find out?

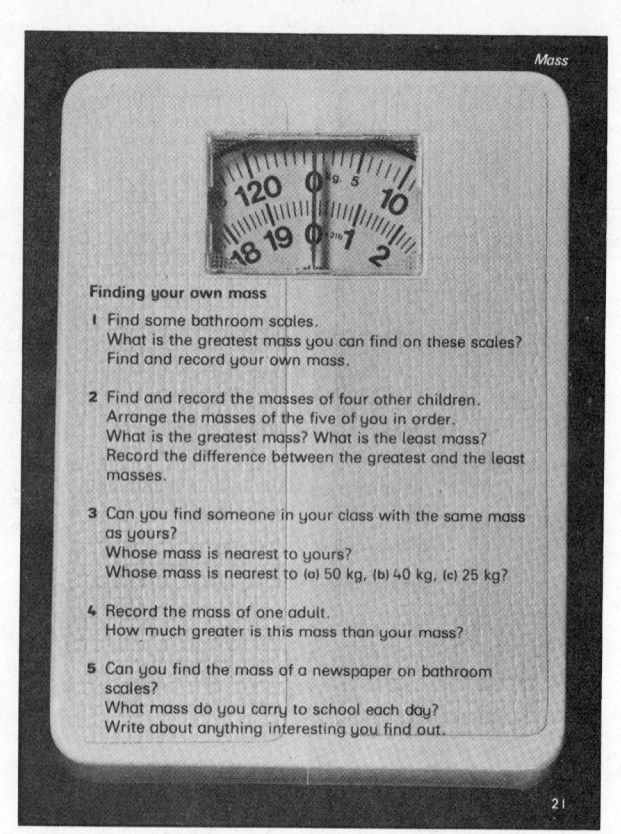

Mass

Finding your own mass

1. Find some bathroom scales.
   What is the greatest mass you can find on these scales?
   Find and record your own mass.

2. Find and record the masses of four other children.
   Arrange the masses of the five of you in order.
   What is the greatest mass? What is the least mass?
   Record the difference between the greatest and the least masses.

3. Can you find someone in your class with the same mass as yours?
   Whose mass is nearest to yours?
   Whose mass is nearest to (a) 50 kg, (b) 40 kg, (c) 25 kg?

4. Record the mass of one adult.
   How much greater is this mass than your mass?

5. Can you find the mass of a newspaper on bathroom scales?
   What mass do you carry to school each day?
   Write about anything interesting you find out.

Notes

1. The elastic bands should be 25–30 cm long and identical. A clean piece of paper should be pasted on the ruler or box to act as a scale.

2. The largest mass which can be supported is just less than the mass which breaks the elastic band. If the bands are too strong, breaking point may not be reached.

3. *Extend* by letting the children use elastic bands of different strengths and making comparisons.

4. Provide, or ask the children to bring, springs or spring scales which work in different ways, eg extension (like elastic bands), compression (bedsprings, hair rollers). Discuss the differences.

Page 21 Finding your own mass

Content
Using bathroom scales to find masses.

Vocabulary
compression scales

Equipment
bathroom scales, newspapers, compression springs (eg hair rollers)

Notes

1. Check that the marker on the scales points to 0, and that the maximum mass can be seen on the scale.

2. Precede by discussing the scales with a group of children. Ask them to find a spring which works in the same way as the bathroom scales. Ask them what each small division measures ($\frac{1}{2}$ kg or 1 kg).

3. *Extend* by asking the children (a) to find an object which just registers on the scale (a standard-sized newspaper does not move the scale), (b) to collect the masses of everyone in the class; they can arrange the masses in order and write about interesting discoveries; (c) to find (and record) objects whose mass can be found on bathroom scales, eg a pile of books, a satchel or case and contents.

Worksheet 3 provides practice and consolidation.

Answers
1 (a) William   (b) John   (c) 12 kg   (d) 112 kg
  (e) 116 kg   (f) 4 kg   (g) 228 kg
  (h) Mary and Alan   (i) 38 kg

Number

Pages 22 and 23 Triangular numbers

Content
Making and working with triangular numbers. Application of triangular numbers. Finding that two consecutive triangular numbers added together make a square number.

Vocabulary
triangular number, sequence

Equipment
counters or other identical counting material

Notes

1. The triangular number shown on the lorry has 10 pipes. The next smallest number is 6. The next is 3. The smallest of all is 1.

2. The first six triangular numbers are   1 3 6 10 15 21
   The differences are   2 3 4 5 6
   These are counting numbers.

3. The next triangular numbers are 28 and 36. The difference pattern is 7 and 8.

4. Triangular numbers can also be made by adding the counting numbers: 1, 1 + 2, 1 + 2 + 3, 1 + 2 + 3 + 4, 1 + 2 + 3 + 4 + 5, etc.

Q4 The picture should look like this. 50 is not a triangular number.

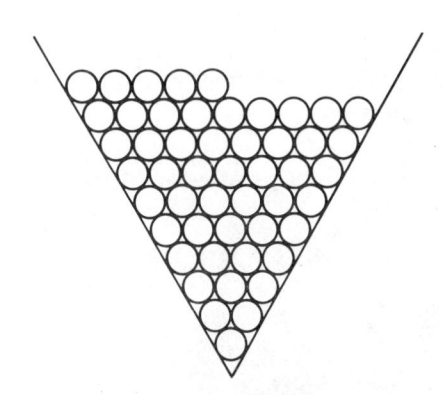

Q5 Some children will need apparatus to build up the number 100 to see if it is a triangular number. Others will be able to build on the patterns already found: 1, 3, 6, 10, 15, ... 100 is not a triangular number.

Number

Triangular numbers

1. Look at the pipes on this lorry. The ends make a triangular shape. Use counters to make the same triangular shape.

   How many did you use? This number is a triangular number.
   What is the next smaller triangular number? And the next one?
   And the smallest of all?
   Make the numbers which continue this sequence, using counters.
   Make a list of all the numbers in your sequence.

2. Write down the first six triangular numbers. Find the difference between each pair.

   1   3   6   10
     2   3   4

   What is the pattern? Find the next two triangular numbers.
   Does the pattern continue?

3. Here is another way of making triangular numbers. Make a table to show the pattern of the first eight triangular numbers.

	Triangular number	Number pattern
1st	1	1
2nd	3	1 + 2
3rd	6	1 + 2 + 3
4th		

4. Chemists use triangular numbers to count pills. Is 50 a triangular number? How did you find out? Draw a picture to show how the chemist counts out 50 pills.

5. Is 100 a triangular number? Show how you found out.

6. What is the tenth triangular number? What is the eleventh triangular number?

7. Add the first two triangular numbers together. Then add together any other two triangular numbers that are next to each other. What do you notice? Do this for all the pairs of triangular numbers in order, as shown. Is the sum of each pair a square number?

   1
   + 4
   3
   +
   6
   + ?
   10
   ? +
   15
   +
   21
   +

Q6 55 is the tenth triangular number.
66 is the eleventh triangular number.
(Note: 55 + 11 = 66)

Q7 1 + 3 = 4
When any two consecutive triangular numbers are added together the result is a square number, eg 10 + 15 = 25, 55 + 66 = 121.
Encourage several attempts at adding consecutive numbers before the children are asked to comment on their results. Test out their ideas with larger triangular numbers.

Page 24 Pocket money

Content
Using the four operations with pocket money.

Vocabulary
construction

Equipment
coins (5p to 50p), dice

Notes
Q1 Most children will give their answers in pence.
Amount saved in (a) *2 weeks*: Joanne 70p, Warren 60p, Clare 50p, Kevin 40p
(b) *3 weeks*: Joanne £1.05, Warren 90p, Clare 75p, Kevin 60p
(c) *5 weeks*: Joanne £1.75, Warren £1.50, Clare £1.25, Kevin £1.00
(d) *7 weeks*: Joanne £2.45, Warren £2.10, Clare £1.75, Kevin £1.40
(e) *10 weeks*: Joanne £3.50, Warren £3.00, Clare £2.50, Kevin £2.00
Notice how the children find the answers to Q1 and see if any use the earlier totals to help them find new totals, eg total for 2 weeks and 3 weeks = total for 5 weeks.

Q2 Time taken to save £1: Joanne, 3 weeks; Warren, 4 weeks; Clare, 4 weeks; Kevin, 5 weeks

Q3 Some children will need to take Joanne's and Kevin's pocket money and share it out. Others will see that Joanne has to give Kevin 7½p.
Extend by asking how much money Warren has to give Clare so that they have the same amount (and for other pairs of children).

Q4 Some children will work from the answer to Q1 to find out how long it takes Warren to save for the kit. Others will add 35p successively or work from £3.50 (ten weeks).
It takes 15 weeks.

Q5 When playing the pocket money game, make sure that the children keep a running total.

Page 25 A hundreds game

Content
Making 3-digit numbers by throwing three dice; arranging the numbers in order. Finding the highest and lowest possible scores.

Equipment
dice

Notes
1. This game provides an opportunity for listening to the children reading the

THE Hundreds Game

Work with a partner. Use three dice of different sizes.

The largest one shows the number of hundreds.

The middle one shows the number of tens.

The smallest one shows the number of ones.

Both throw all the dice at once and record the number. Do this six times each.
Arrange your own numbers in order from the smallest to the largest.
Score 1 point for each 100.
Whose score was higher?
The chart on the right shows how points are recorded.
What would be the highest number for one throw?
What would be the lowest?
If you threw a number in the 600s for every one of six throws, how many points would you score?
Play the game five times. Who won more games?

Number	Points
123	1
211	2
245	2
334	3
451	4
612	6
Total	18

Number

Making different numbers

1 2 3 4 5 6 7 8 9

1 Take a set of cards numbered 1 to 9. Shuffle them. Place them face down and take three cards.
Use all three cards each time. Make as many 3-digit numbers as you can. Record these numbers.
Could you make six different numbers?
Record your numbers in order of size. Put the smallest number first.

2 Make a zero card.
Use it with two others to make 3-digit numbers.
How many different numbers can you make this time?
Arrange these in order with the smallest first.

3 Use the numbers 8 8 3 to make 3-digit numbers.
How many can you find?
Try with these numbers. 5 5 2

4 If all three number cards are the same, how many different numbers can you make?

5 How many different numbers can you make with two cards only?

numbers, eg 123 as one hundred and twenty-three.

2. Discuss the order with individual children, eg when the first two digits are the same, ask, 'How did you decide the order of these two numbers?'

Q3 The highest point total is 36, if a number in the 600s was scored at every throw.

3. *Extend* by scoring according to (a) the total of the digits, (b) the differences between the hundreds score and the units score (18 − 16 = 2, in the table given).

Page 26 Making different numbers

Content
Making 3-digit numbers from a random selection of cards; arranging these in order of size.

Equipment
cards numbers 0 to 9

Notes
Q1 There are six possible answers.

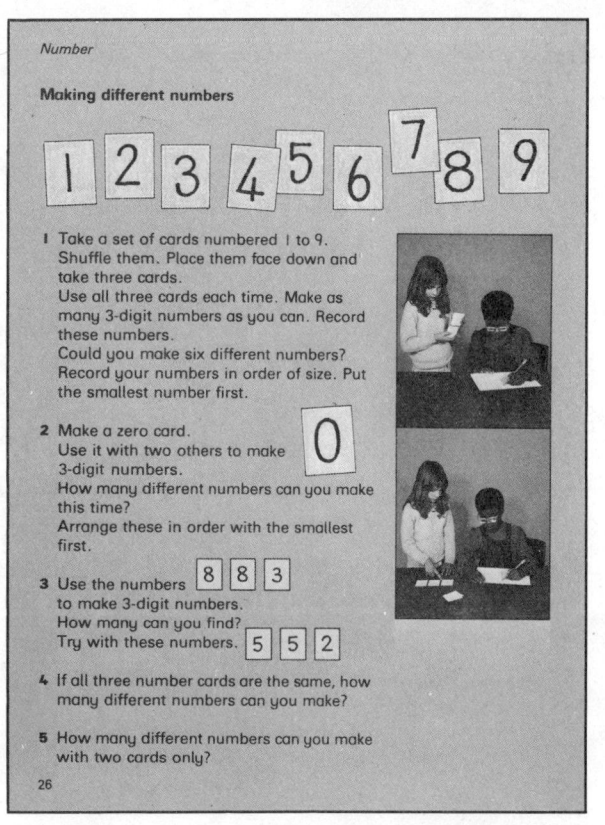

Q2 Discuss with the groups if numbers like 023 are to be allowed. If 023 etc is not allowed, there are four answers.

Q3 Three answers.

Q4 One number.

Q5 Two numbers if the cards are different; one number if the cards are the same or include a zero.

Extend by asking how many different numbers can be made from the digits 1, 4, 7 if the numbers can have one digit, two digits or three digits (3 + 6 + 6 = 15 numbers).
Repeat with three digits, two of which are the same.

Worksheet 4 provides practice in working with 3-digit numbers, and also with multiplication.

Answers
1 The 3-digit numbers are:
234, 243, 324, 342, 423, 432
(a) 432, 234 (b) 666 (c) 198
(d) 243, 423
(e) 234, 324, 342, 432

2 (a) 6, 15, 18, 24 (b) 8, 16, 20, 24
(c) 10, 15, 20, 35 (d) 12, 18, 24, 30, 36

Page 27 A pairs game

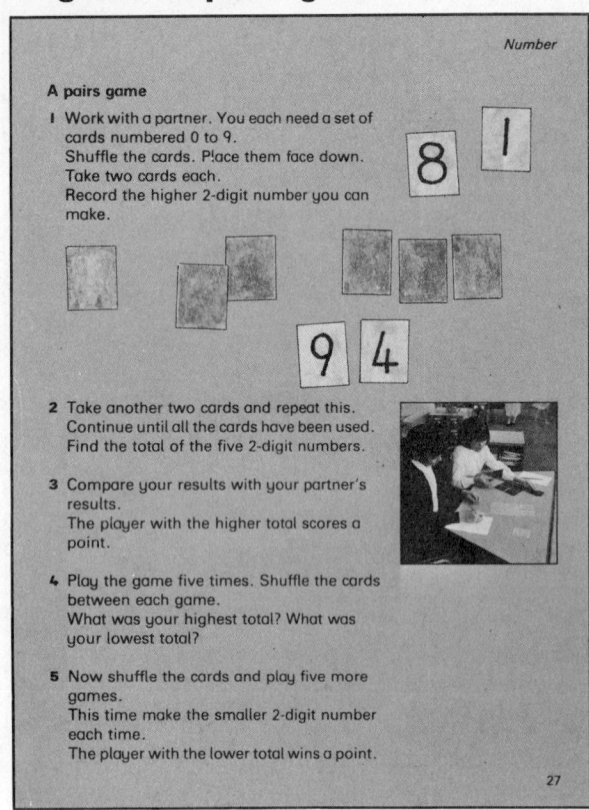

> Number
>
> **A pairs game**
>
> 1. Work with a partner. You each need a set of cards numbered 0 to 9.
>   Shuffle the cards. Place them face down.
>   Take two cards each.
>   Record the higher 2-digit number you can make.
>
> 2. Take another two cards and repeat this.
>   Continue until all the cards have been used.
>   Find the total of the five 2-digit numbers.
>
> 3. Compare your results with your partner's results.
>   The player with the higher total scores a point.
>
> 4. Play the game five times. Shuffle the cards between each game.
>   What was your highest total? What was your lowest total?
>
> 5. Now shuffle the cards and play five more games.
>   This time make the smaller 2-digit number each time.
>   The player with the lower total wins a point.

Content
Making 2-digit numbers from pairs of cards, 0 to 9, randomly selected.

Equipment
cards numbered 0 to 9

Notes
1. Check that the numbers are being recorded correctly.

2. Try to observe if any children use the pattern of the numbers to help them add, eg 6 and 4, 1 and 9, etc.

3. *Extend* with some children by asking what is the highest possible total and the lowest possible total. Highest total 360. Lowest total 135 if 0 is used in the tens column. Discuss the strategies used. Some children may begin 98, 76, ... but this does not give the highest total – the five highest numbers must be used for the tens.

Page 28 Find the fractions

> Number
>
> **Find the fractions**
>
> 1. Take three strips of paper of equal length.
>   Find one half of one strip.
>   How many half pieces make the whole strip?
>   Write $\frac{1}{2}$ in each part.
>
> | 1 whole strip |
> |---|
>
> | $\frac{1}{2}$ | $\frac{1}{2}$ |
> |---|---|
>
> 2. Divide the second strip into four equal parts.
>   Find one quarter of the strip.
>   How many quarter pieces make the whole strip?
>   Write $\frac{1}{4}$ in each part.
>
> | $\frac{1}{4}$ | $\frac{1}{4}$ | $\frac{1}{4}$ | $\frac{1}{4}$ |
> |---|---|---|---|
>
> 3. Use your strips to find how many quarters make a half.
>   Copy and complete these.
>   (a) $\frac{1}{2} + \frac{1}{2} =$
>   (b) $\frac{1}{4} + \frac{1}{4} + \frac{1}{4} + \frac{1}{4} =$
>
> 5. Write three-quarters as a fraction.
>
> 6. Cut off $\frac{1}{2}$ from your first strip. What fraction is left?
>   Cut off $\frac{1}{4}$ from your second strip. What fraction is left?

Content
Addition and subtraction of simple fractions.

Equipment
paper strips

Notes
1. Make sure that the children find half (and quarter) of a strip by folding rather than measuring, (but try to avoid telling them what to do).

2. Ask the following questions:
   (a) If you had cut off $\frac{3}{4}$ from the second strip, what fraction would be left?
   (b) Copy and complete: $1 - \frac{1}{2} =$
   $1 - \frac{1}{4} =$
   $1 - \frac{3}{4} =$
   (c) Take three sheets of paper. Divide one into halves and another into quarters. Label all the parts.
   Write all you can about these fractions.

3. Not all the children will divide the paper into parts in the same way, so be prepared for a

variety of shapes. Encourage the children to find out as much as they can about these fractions.

Page 29 Half a glass

> **Half a glass**
>
> 1 Work with a partner.
> Find eight identical plastic glasses.
> Fill three of the glasses with water.
> Label one of these 'I whole glass'.
>
> 2 Divide the second glassful into halves. How many glasses did you use for halves?
> Divide the third glassful into quarters. How many glasses did you use for quarters?
> Label all these glasses.
>
> 3 Find the answers to these questions. Use your whole, half and quarter glasses of water.
>
> (a) If you pour $\frac{1}{4}$ glass into $\frac{1}{2}$ glass, will it fill the glass? What fraction still needs to be filled?
>
> (b) If you pour $\frac{3}{4}$ glass into $\frac{3}{4}$ glass, will it overflow?
>
> (c) If you pour $\frac{1}{2}$ glass into $\frac{3}{4}$ glass, will it overflow?
>
> (d) You have $\frac{1}{2}$ glass of water. Your friend has $\frac{3}{4}$ glass. What fraction has she more than you?
>
> (e) If your friend has $\frac{1}{4}$ glass, what fraction has she less than you?
>
> (f) Drink $\frac{1}{2}$ glass from the whole glass. How much is left?

Content
Continuation of work with halves and quarters.

Equipment
identical near-clear plastic glasses, sticky paper (for labels)

Notes
Q3 (a) It will not fill the glass. $\frac{1}{4}$ more needs to be added.
  (b) It will overflow.
  (c) This will overflow as well.
  (d) $\frac{1}{4}$ glass. Ask the children to show you this answer.
  (e) $\frac{1}{4}$ glass. Again, ask the children to prove it.
  (f) $\frac{1}{2}$ glass.

Extend by asking the children to work these fractions:

$\frac{1}{4} + \frac{1}{4} =$ $\frac{1}{2} + \frac{1}{4} =$

$\frac{1}{4} + \frac{1}{4} + \frac{1}{4} =$ $\frac{3}{4} - \frac{1}{4} =$

$\frac{3}{4} + \frac{1}{4} =$ $\frac{3}{4} - \frac{1}{2} =$

Worksheet 5 gives practice in working with quarters and thirds.

Pages 30 and 31 Nuts!

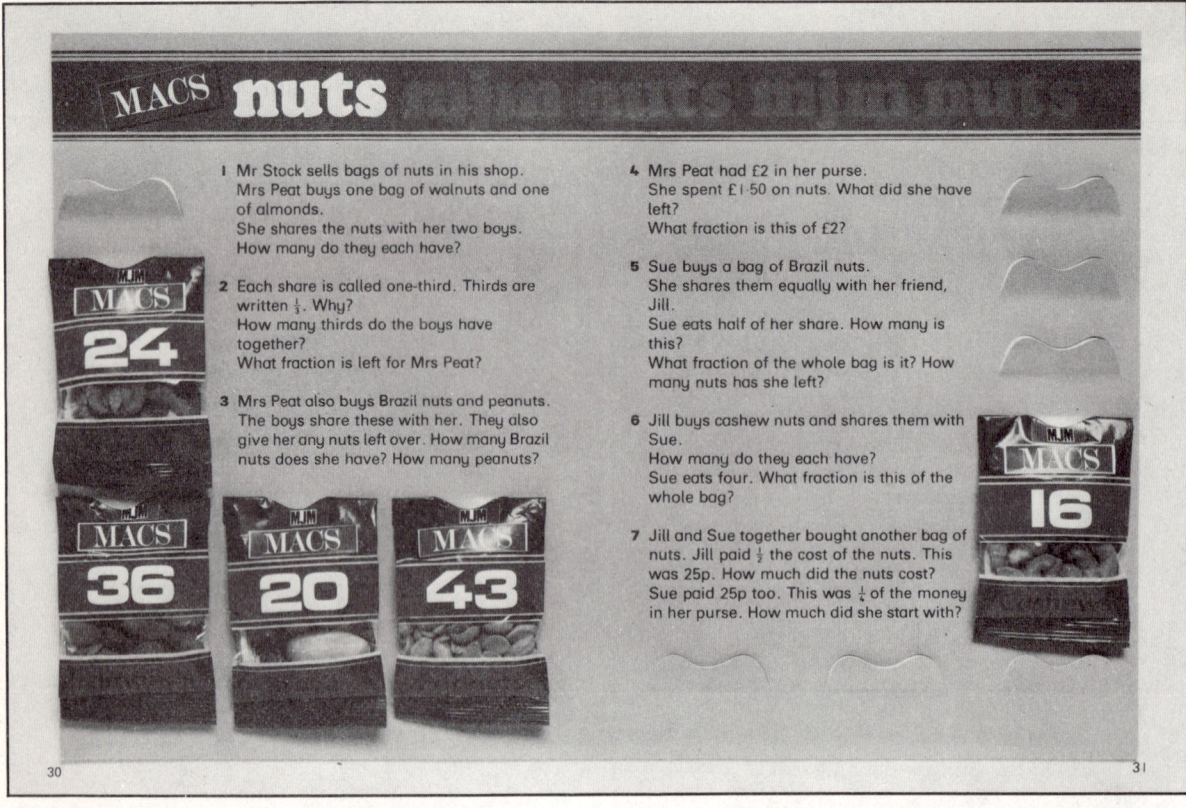

MACS nuts

1. Mr Stock sells bags of nuts in his shop. Mrs Peat buys one bag of walnuts and one of almonds.
She shares the nuts with her two boys. How many do they each have?

2. Each share is called one-third. Thirds are written $\frac{1}{3}$. Why?
How many thirds do the boys have together?
What fraction is left for Mrs Peat?

3. Mrs Peat also buys Brazil nuts and peanuts. The boys share these with her. They also give her any nuts left over. How many Brazil nuts does she have? How many peanuts?

4. Mrs Peat had £2 in her purse. She spent £1·50 on nuts. What did she have left?
What fraction is this of £2?

5. Sue buys a bag of Brazil nuts. She shares them equally with her friend, Jill.
Sue eats half of her share. How many is this?
What fraction of the whole bag is it? How many nuts has she left?

6. Jill buys cashew nuts and shares them with Sue.
How many do they each have?
Sue eats four. What fraction is this of the whole bag?

7. Jill and Sue together bought another bag of nuts. Jill paid $\frac{1}{2}$ the cost of the nuts. This was 25p. How much did the nuts cost?
Sue paid 25p too. This was $\frac{1}{4}$ of the money in her purse. How much did she start with?

(Bags shown: 24, 36, 20, 43, 16)

Content
Introducing thirds and finding thirds of given numbers. Finding half and quarter of certain amounts; application with money.

Vocabulary
one-third, thirds

Equipment
counters or unit cubes, coins

Notes

Q1 If necessary, let the children share out the 24 walnuts and 36 almonds into three piles. They all have 20 each – 8 walnuts and 12 almonds.

Q2 The children should answer, '$\frac{1}{3}$ is one part of 3'. The boys have $\frac{2}{3}$ between them, and Mrs Peat has $\frac{1}{3}$.

Q3 Mrs Peat has 6 brazils and 2 left over. She has 14 peanuts and the 1 left over.

Q4 After buying the nuts Mrs Peat has 50p left ($\frac{1}{4}$ of £2).

Q5 5, $\frac{1}{4}$, 5

Q6 8, $\frac{1}{4}$

Q7 50p, £1

Extend this work by asking the children to make up problems of their own, similar to the ones on these pages.

Shape

Pages 32 and 33 Introducing shape

Content
Checking that the children can (a) understand the vocabulary associated with familiar 3D shapes and their faces; (b) recall how to make the net of an open cube and find its volume; (c) recognise angles of different sizes and when a frame is rigid; (d) make mirror and rotational patterns.

Vocabulary
cuboid, cylinder, cone, rigid, sphere, net, face, edge, corner, angle, right-angle, horizontal, vertical, hollow

Equipment
cone, cube, cuboid, cylinder, ball (sphere), 2-centimetre squared paper, centimetre squared paper, scissors, sellotape, centimetre cubes, coloured pencils, boards, drawing pins (Q5)

Notes
Q1 Precede by making sure that the children can name all the shapes, and are familiar with the vocabulary. Introduce the word 'sphere'. When children come across new shapes, they should add these to the table — eg pyramids and prisms.
If an open cube is not available, suggest that the children imagine a hollow cube with the lid removed (or make one from squared paper).
Extend this work by asking the children to name the shapes of the faces.

Q2 Precede by discussing the information about an open cube from the table in Q1. Encourage the children to make nets of different patterns. Ask, 'Have any of the patterns mirror symmetry? How many different patterns (nets) can you make with mirror symmetry?' (three).
The open cube should hold two layers of four cubes (eight in all). If the finished open cube is too small to take the centimetre cubes, suggest that the children use centimetre cubes to make a model of the open cube.

Shape

Introducing shape

1 Find one of each of these shapes.
  cone, cube, cuboid, cylinder, sphere (ball).
  Make and complete a table like this.

Name	Number of flat faces	Number of curved faces	Number of straight edges	Number of curved edges	Number of corners
Cone	1	1	0	1	1
Cube					
Cuboid					
Cylinder					
Sphere					
Open cube					

2 Use squared paper to cut the net of an open cube of edge 2 centimetres. Fold it to find whether your net makes an open cube. If so, cut an identical net.
Use sellotape to make one net into an open cube.
Estimate how many centimetre cubes your cube will hold.
Use centimetre cubes to check.
On squared paper, draw the net of a closed cube.
Cut it out and fold it to check that you are right.

3. (a) These are bridges made of bars bolted together. Copy them. Which bridge would be strongest?
(b) Show how you could make the others stronger.
(c) Copy the bridges again.
Colour vertical lines in red and horizontal lines in blue.
Colour in green all the angles which are not right-angles.

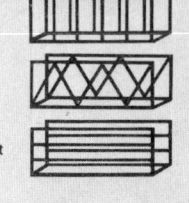

4 Copy this pattern on to centimetre squared paper.
Colour it.
Draw the reflection.
Check whether you are right.

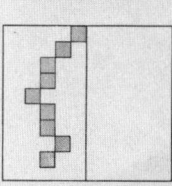

5 Work with a friend.
From 2-centimetre squared paper cut a triangle like this. Pin the triangle near its centre, to a sheet of plain paper.
Draw round it.
Turn the triangle through a small angle.
Draw round it again.
Continue turning the triangle and drawing round it until you get back to the start.
Mark in all the right-angles.

On another sheet of paper use your triangle to make a mirror pattern. How did you do this?

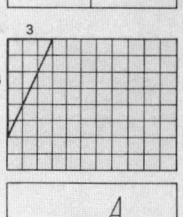

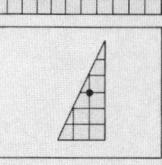

Q3 (ii), in which the frame is made of triangles, is the strongest because the component triangles are rigid.
(i) can be made rigid by using diagonal bars.
(iii) can be made rigid by using one diagonal bar as in a five-bar gate.
(ii) is the only frame with angles other than right-angles.

Q4 Precede by asking the children to rule in the mirror line (on a thick line near the middle of the paper). Ask them to tell you how they can check to see whether they are right.

Q5 The cut triangle should be fixed with a drawing pin to a sheet of paper on a board. Suggest that the children colour the patterns, and display them.

Extend by asking the children to mark in the outline of the triangle in the quarter-turn positions (see figure). Ask them to show two triangles in the half-turn positions. Ask, 'How do you know that this pattern is a rotational pattern?' (the triangles all have the same face up). Let them make and colour other rotational patterns. In order to make a mirror pattern with the triangle, the triangle must be turned over as shown below.

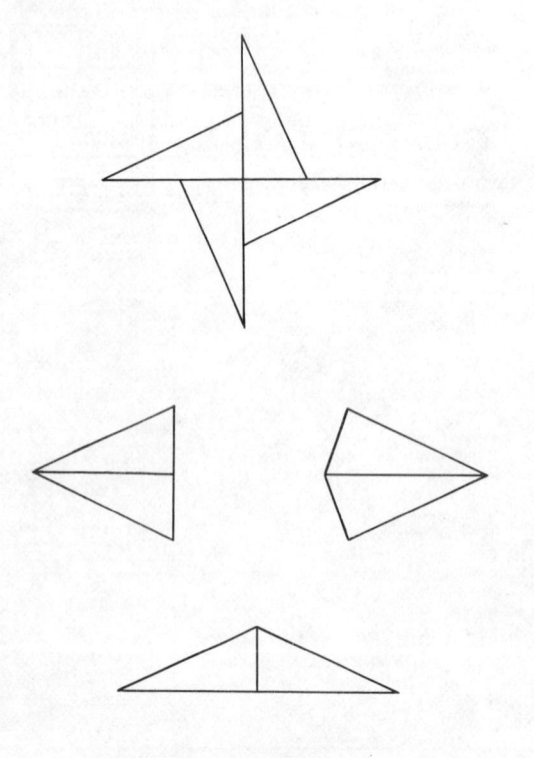

Page 34 Making mirror patterns

Content
Finding and making patterns with mirror symmetry.

Vocabulary
mirror symmetry, mirror line (axis), fabric

Equipment
fabrics or wrapping paper with repeating patterns, unbreakable mirrors, scissors, paint and brushes

Notes
1. Precede by asking the children to bring fabrics or wrapping paper with repeating patterns. Ask them to find the mirror patterns.

2. Unbreakable mirrors can be obtained from Osmiroid Educational, E.S. Perry Ltd, Osmiroid Works, Gosport, Hants PO13 0AL.

3. The children should check the patterns using mirrors. They should mount the cut-outs and the patterns they make.

4. *Extend* by letting the children make patterns using paint between the folds rather than cutting.

Page 35 Mirror symmetry

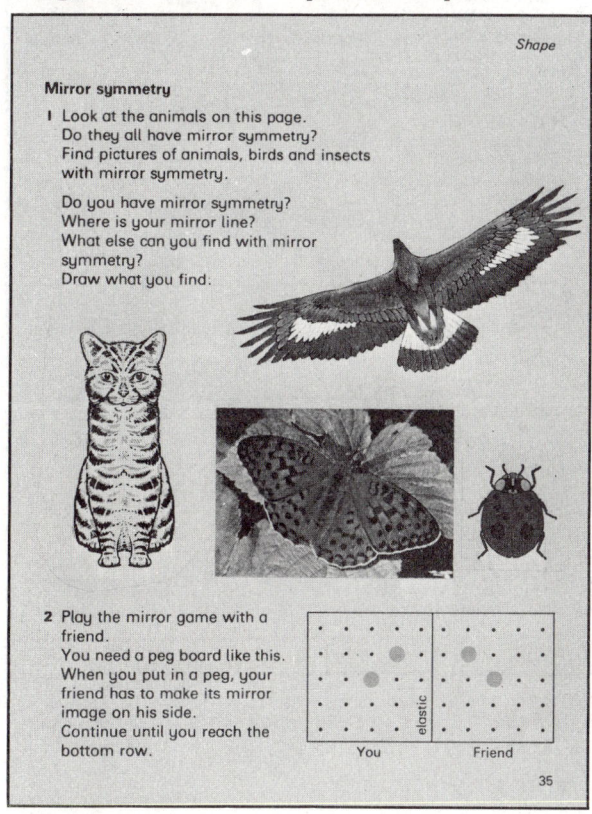

Content
Practice in recognising and making patterns with mirror symmetry.

Vocabulary
mirror image

Equipment
pictures of animals and birds etc with mirror symmetry, peg boards, coloured pegs, squared paper, coloured pencils

Notes
1. In the book corner, focus attention on insects, animals, fish and birds with mirror symmetry. On three-dimensional objects, the mirror 'line' is really a plane — the mirror itself.

2. The peg boards should not have more than 10 rows of holes. The mirror lines should be marked down the centre of the board. At first the children should use one colour only. Later on, they should be given different coloured pegs and asked to match pegs of the same colour on either side of the board. The children do not find diagonal moves easy, and need plenty of practice with these.

3. Ask, 'How do you know where to put the mirror peg?' ('It is in the same row'. It is the same number of holes from the mirror line'.)

4. *Variation.* Use squared paper folded in half and coloured pens or pencils. This can be an individual activity or played by pairs of children.

Pages 36 and 37 Make a mobile

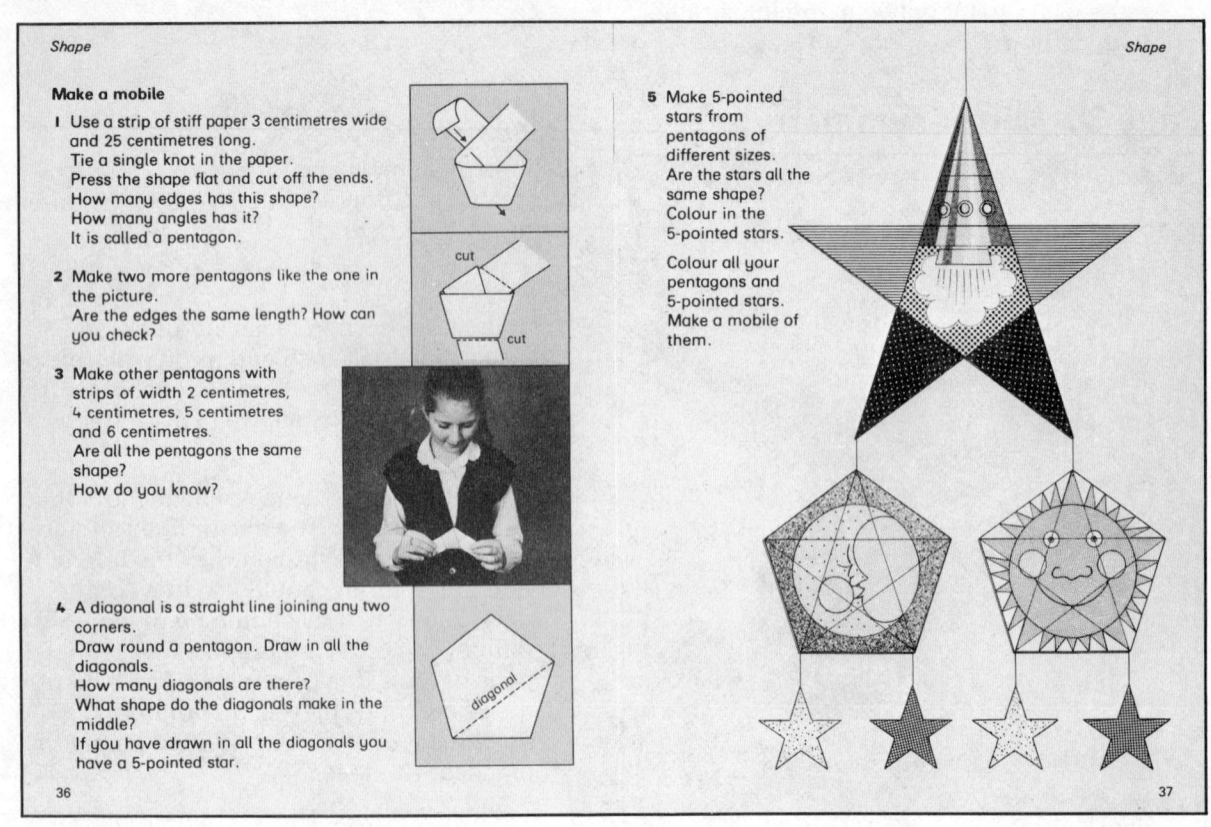

Shape

Make a mobile

1. Use a strip of stiff paper 3 centimetres wide and 25 centimetres long.
   Tie a single knot in the paper.
   Press the shape flat and cut off the ends.
   How many edges has this shape?
   How many angles has it?
   It is called a pentagon.

2. Make two more pentagons like the one in the picture.
   Are the edges the same length? How can you check?

3. Make other pentagons with strips of width 2 centimetres, 4 centimetres, 5 centimetres and 6 centimetres.
   Are all the pentagons the same shape?
   How do you know?

4. A diagonal is a straight line joining any two corners.
   Draw round a pentagon. Draw in all the diagonals.
   How many diagonals are there?
   What shape do the diagonals make in the middle?
   If you have drawn in all the diagonals you have a 5-pointed star.

Shape

5. Make 5-pointed stars from pentagons of different sizes.
   Are the stars all the same shape?
   Colour in the 5-pointed stars.

   Colour all your pentagons and 5-pointed stars.
   Make a mobile of them.

Content
Making regular pentagons of different sizes by tying a knot in a strip of paper. Making 5-pointed stars by joining diagonals.

Vocabulary
diagonal, pentagon, 5-pointed star
You may like to discuss with some children the meaning of prefixes, quad ..., pent..., hex..., oct..., and ask for other examples.

Equipment
stiff paper strips, paint, thick brushes, rulers, scissors

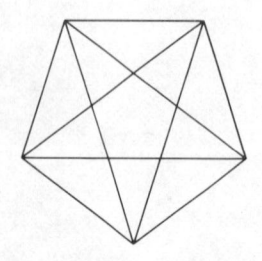

Notes

1. The strips of stiff paper, should be of widths 2 cm, 3 cm and 4 cm (all 25 cm long), 5 cm and 6 cm (both 40 cm long).

2. Make sure that the knot is made carefully so that the pentagons are regular, with edges all the same length and angles the same size.

3. The children can check that edge lengths are the same by putting the pentagons one on top of the other, matching edges and angles, and rotating to a new position.

4. There should be two diagonals from each corner. The shape in the middle of the star is a smaller regular pentagon.

Worksheet 6 provides extension work with shapes and their diagonals. For example, the number of diagonals from each corner of a hexagon is 3. The total number of diagonals is $\frac{1}{2}$ of $6 \times 3 = 9$.

Pages 38 and 39 Box shapes

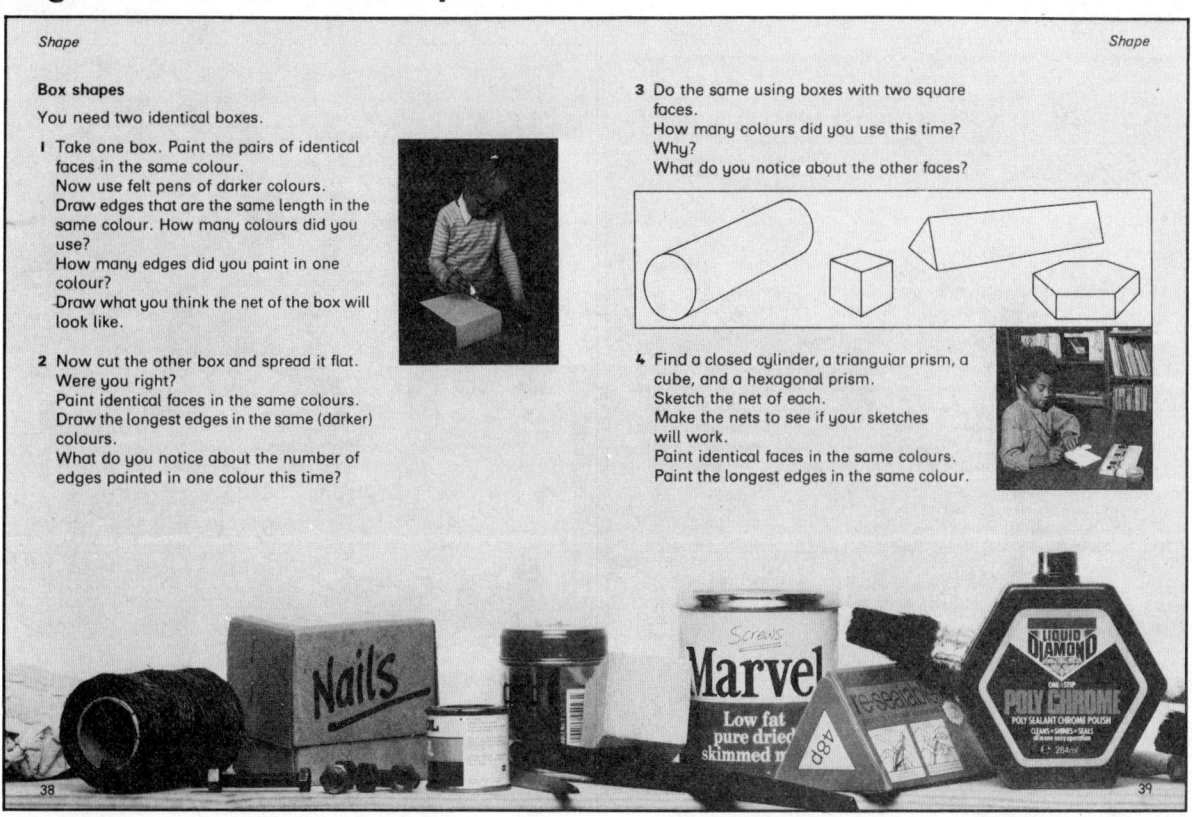

Content
Studying 3-dimensional shapes and making their nets.

Vocabulary
hexagon, prism

Equipment
pairs of identical cuboids, closed cylinders, triangular prisms, cubes, hexagonal prisms, paint and felt pens (5 colours), brushes, scissors

Notes
1. Ask the children to collect pairs of identical cuboids (small breakfast cereal containers are ideal). The children should also help to collect other shapes, if possible in identical pairs.

Q1 Ask the children to look carefully at the box and to draw what they think the box will look like when it is cut and laid flat.

Q2 Before the children cut the second box to lay it flat on the table, ask them to cut off the flaps which help to keep the box closed. Check that they have done this correctly.

Ask the children, 'Are all the nets alike?'. Discuss the different patterns. Ask the children to sort these into sets according to the patterns of the nets; eg a windmill pattern, patterns with mirror symmetry.

Q3 Repeat the questions for the nets made on page 39. If two identical shapes are available, mount the 3-dimensional shape with its net.

Worksheet 7 provides further work on making nets.

Answers
A makes a square-based pyramid, B a triangular-based pyramid (tetrahedron), C an open-ended cylinder and D a triangular prism.

Length

Page 40 Introducing length

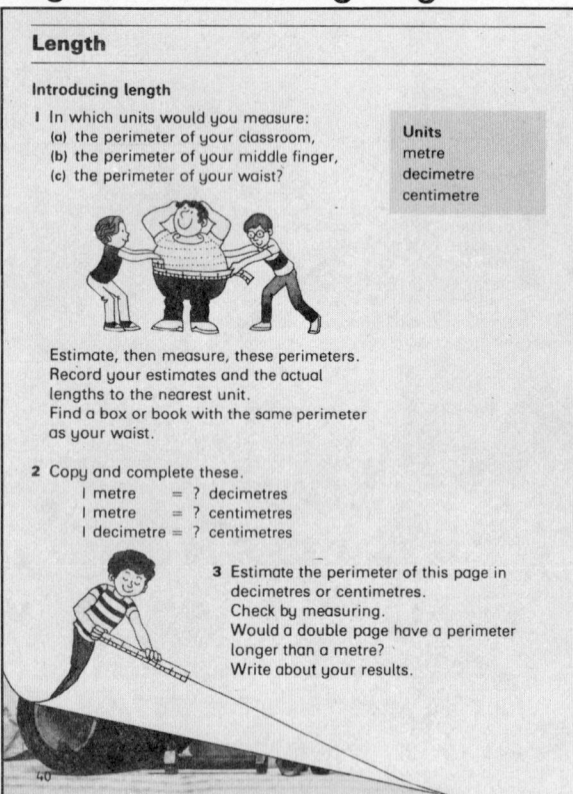

> **Length**
>
> **Introducing length**
>
> 1 In which units would you measure:
>   (a) the perimeter of your classroom,
>   (b) the perimeter of your middle finger,
>   (c) the perimeter of your waist?
>
> **Units**
> metre
> decimetre
> centimetre
>
> Estimate, then measure, these perimeters.
> Record your estimates and the actual
> lengths to the nearest unit.
> Find a box or book with the same perimeter
> as your waist.
>
> 2 Copy and complete these.
>   1 metre = ? decimetres
>   1 metre = ? centimetres
>   1 decimetre = ? centimetres
>
> 3 Estimate the perimeter of this page in
>   decimetres or centimetres.
>   Check by measuring.
>   Would a double page have a perimeter
>   longer than a metre?
>   Write about your results.

Content
Checking that the children (a) know the appropriate units of length; (b) can use the units for measuring length; (c) know the relationship between successive standard units of length.

Vocabulary
centimetre, decimetre, metre

Equipment
metre strips marked at 5 cm intervals, boxes, books, etc for measuring.

Notes
Q1 Check that the children measure to the nearest unit. Discuss part-units (halves or quarters) with them when they have finished.

Q3 When measuring the perimeter of a double page, only the outer edges should be included.

Page 41 Make a 2-metre measure

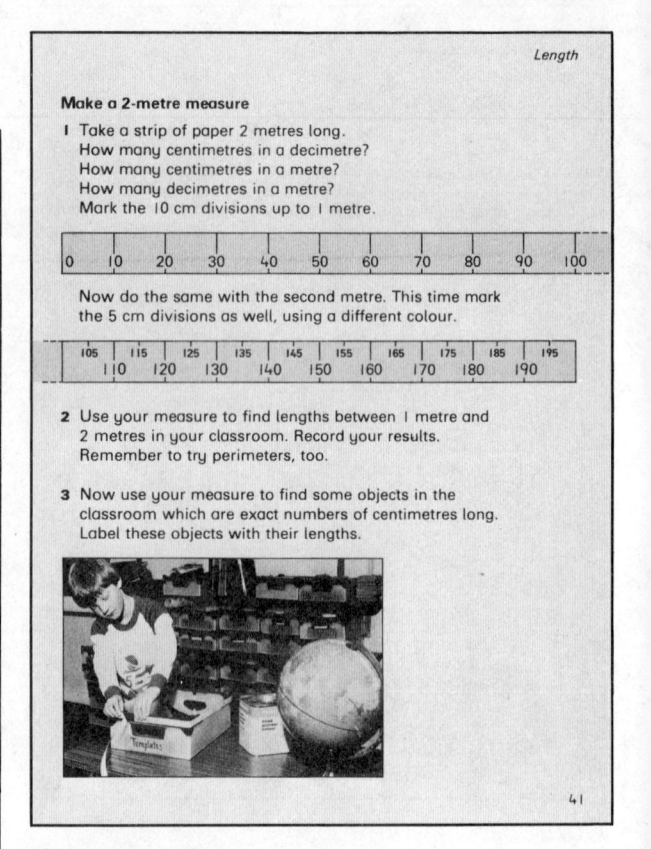

> **Make a 2-metre measure**
>
> 1 Take a strip of paper 2 metres long.
>   How many centimetres in a decimetre?
>   How many centimetres in a metre?
>   How many decimetres in a metre?
>   Mark the 10 cm divisions up to 1 metre.
>
> | 0 | 10 | 20 | 30 | 40 | 50 | 60 | 70 | 80 | 90 | 100 |
>
> Now do the same with the second metre. This time mark
> the 5 cm divisions as well, using a different colour.
>
> | 105 | 115 | 125 | 135 | 145 | 155 | 165 | 175 | 185 | 195 |
> | 110 | 120 | 130 | 140 | 150 | 160 | 170 | 180 | 190 |
>
> 2 Use your measure to find lengths between 1 metre and
>   2 metres in your classroom. Record your results.
>   Remember to try perimeters, too.
>
> 3 Now use your measure to find some objects in the
>   classroom which are exact numbers of centimetres long.
>   Label these objects with their lengths.

Content
Using centimetres and metres.

Equipment
paper strips 2 metres long and 2 centimetres wide, coloured pencils, objects for measuring

Notes
1. Strips should be on centimetre squared paper.

2. Make sure that some objects or lengths in the classroom are 2 metres long. Include perimeters, eg tables or desks.

3. *Extend* by finding longer distances and lengths, eg 3 metres, 4 metres.

Worksheet 8 provides practice in estimating and measuring in centimetres.

Answers
1 a: 13 cm; b: 7 cm; c: 5 cm; d: 2 cm; e: 6 cm;
   f: 3 cm; g: 9 cm; h: 15 cm

2 h: a and d, e and g;   g: e and f, b and d;
   b: c and d

3 (a) g and e, e and f (b) g and b, h and a, b and c, c and f (c) b and e, e and c, f and d
4 (a) a and d, e and g (b) c and h, a and b

Page 42 How far can you jump

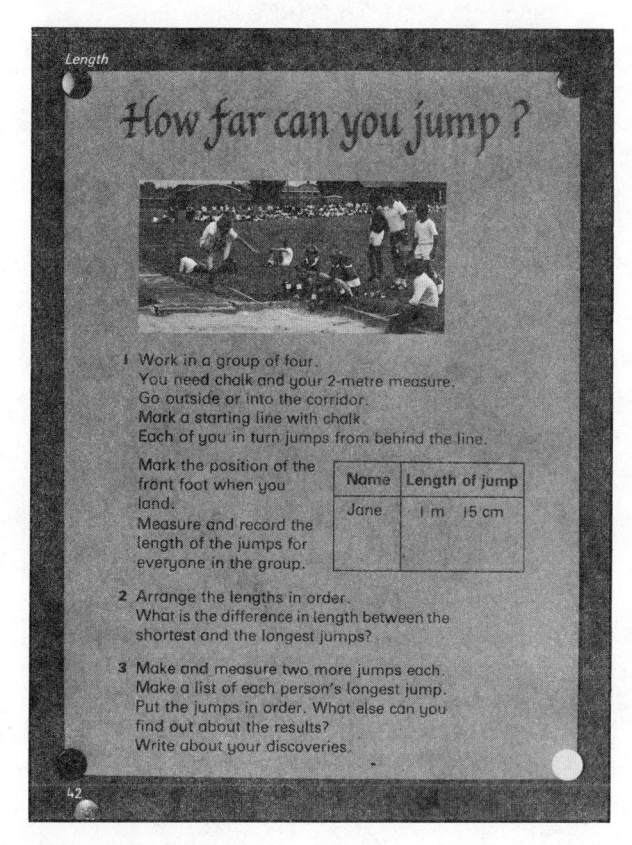

Content
Measuring and arranging long jumps in order, and finding differences.

Equipment
2-metre measures, chalk

Notes
1. Lengths should be measured in metres and centimetres to the nearest centimetre.
2. Children can find differences in lengths directly, using their 2-metre measures (which is an application of shopkeeper's addition), or by decomposition.
3. *Extend* by finding longest strides. Discuss how many of each child's strides should be measured to obtain a sensible estimate of the length of one stride.

Page 43 Making things equal

Content
Introducing the concept of an average length without using the vocabulary.

Equipment
2-metre measures, paper strips, centimetre squared paper, scissors

Notes
1. Observe whether the children find the average height by joining the height strips together and folding. If they do not, give practice in finding a half and a quarter of strips of paper and sheets of paper. Try to avoid suggesting the folding method yourself, but give further practice in folding if necessary.
2. Measurements should be given to the nearest centimetre.
3. *Extend* by finding the average lengths of other measures, eg reach, pace, head and face perimeters.

25

Time

Pages 44 and 45 Introducing time

Content
Checking that the children know the months of the year and the days of the week, can use a calendar, and can tell and record the time in quarter-hours.

Vocabulary
templates

Equipment
centimetre squared paper, clock templates

Notes
Q2 31 days – January, March, May, July, August, October, December.
Shortest month – February.
30 days – April, June, September, November.

Q4 Holidays are calculated on the number of nights. If you leave and return on the same day, you have had 7 or 14 nights. The Adams family return on 15th July. The Browns return on 20th August.

Q5 Saturdays in July – 6th, 13th, 20th, 27th (1985 calendar). The successive dates differ by seven days.

Q6 Shadows measured at:
9.30, 10.00, 10.30, 11.00, 11.30, 12.00, 12.30, 1.00, 1.30, 2.00, 2.30, 3.00, 3.30
If any children have difficulty, give daily practice until they are confident.

Worksheet 9 provides practice in calendar work for those children who need it.

Answers
1 2 – Wednesday, 8 – Tuesday, 13 – Sunday, 24 – Thursday, 26 – Saturday, 30 – Wednesday
Thursdays – 3, 10, 17, 24, 31
Mondays – 7, 14, 21, 28
Fridays – 4, 11, 18, 25
31.12.1984 – Monday; 1.2.1985 – Friday

3 2nd column – 63; 3rd column – 112
Difference – 49 (7 × difference of 7)

Time

Introducing time

1 Which is the first month of the year?
Which is the last month?
Write the months in order.
    November January March April December February
    September May July October June August

2 Which months of the year have 31 days?
Which is the shortest month? Which months have only 30 days?

3 Copy this calendar on to centimetre squared paper.
Fill in all the days of the week for both months.
Which is the last day of July?
Which is the last day of August?

	JULY		AUGUST	
Mon	1			
Tues	2			
Wed	3			
Thu			1	
Fri				
Sat				
Sun				

4 (a) The Adams family go on holiday on 1st July for two weeks. They leave and return on the same day of the week. On which date do they return?
(b) The Brown family go on holiday on 6th August for two weeks. On which date do they return?

5 Package holidays often start on a Saturday.
Write down the dates of all the Saturdays in July.
What do you notice about this sequence of numbers?

6 Some children decide to measure the shadow of a post.
They start at 9.30, and measure the shadow every half hour during the school day.
Write down the times at which the shadow is measured.
School ends at 3.45 in the afternoon.

7 Write down the times on these clocks.

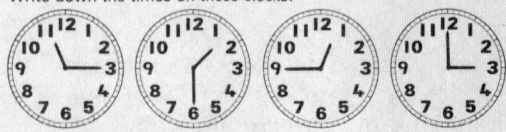

8 Show these times on clock templates.
Paul leaves home at 8.45.
He gets to school at 9 o'clock.
Playtime is at 10.30.
Lunch is at 12.15.

Page 46 Making a minute clock
Page 47 Telling the time in minutes

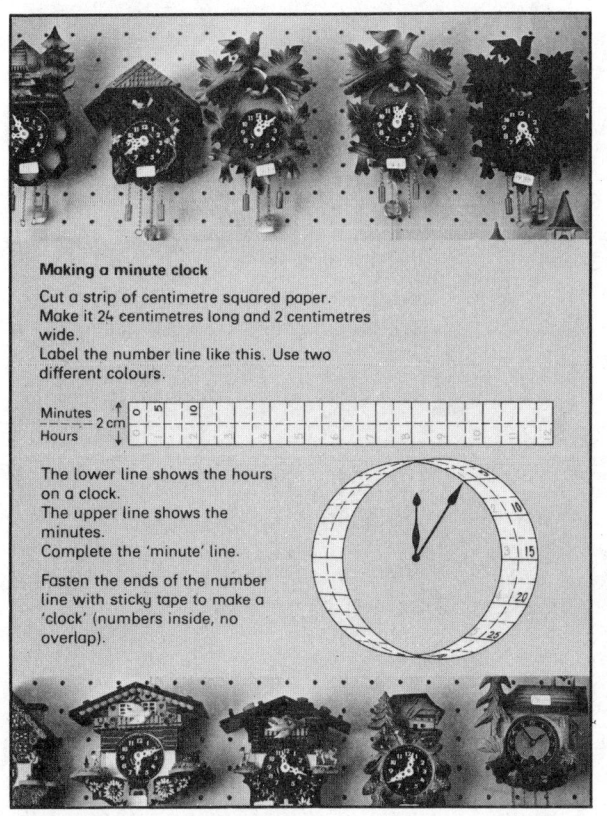

Content
Reading the time at 5-minute intervals.

Vocabulary
overlap

Equipment
stiff paper, coloured pencils, masking tape, clock templates

Notes
1. Stiff paper should be used to make the clock number line. Make sure that the children label this correctly and use two colours. The ends should be joined carefully so that there is no overlap. The number line clock should be vertical with the numbers *inside*.

2. The new 'clocks' can be used with clock templates to help children to read different times for as long as they require this help.

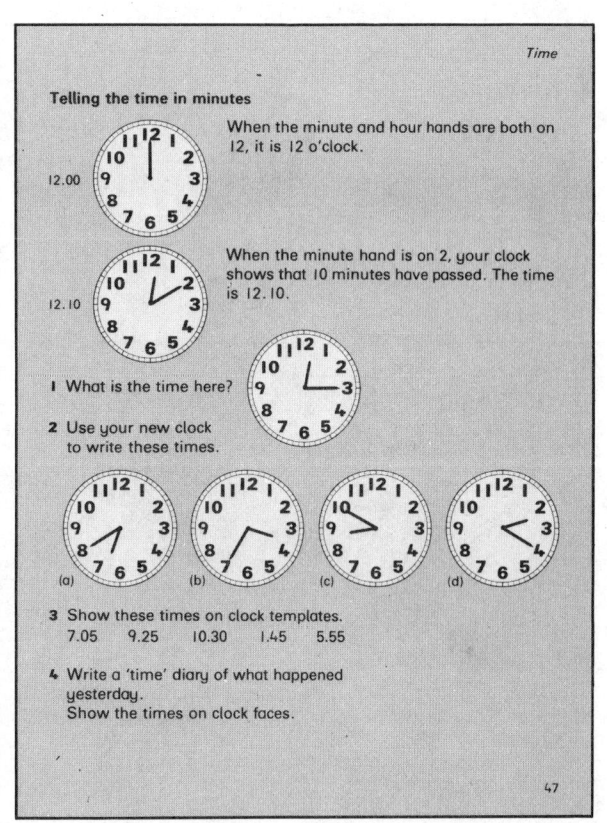

3. Give short daily practice until the children can read the time at any 5-minute interval. Provide plenty of practice (a) in reading the time from clock templates, and (b) in drawing stated times on blank clock templates. Remind the children that the hour hand moves as well as the minute hand!

4. Encourage the children to use times in the stories and diaries they write.

Q1 12.15
Q2 (a) 6.40, (b) 3.35, (c) 8.50, (d) 2.20

Worksheet 10 is a practice page on reading the time at 5-minute intervals.

Answers
1 1.25, 8.10, 2.20, 5.05, 12.35, 6.40, 7.55, 3.50

27

Number

Page 48 Halves and quarters

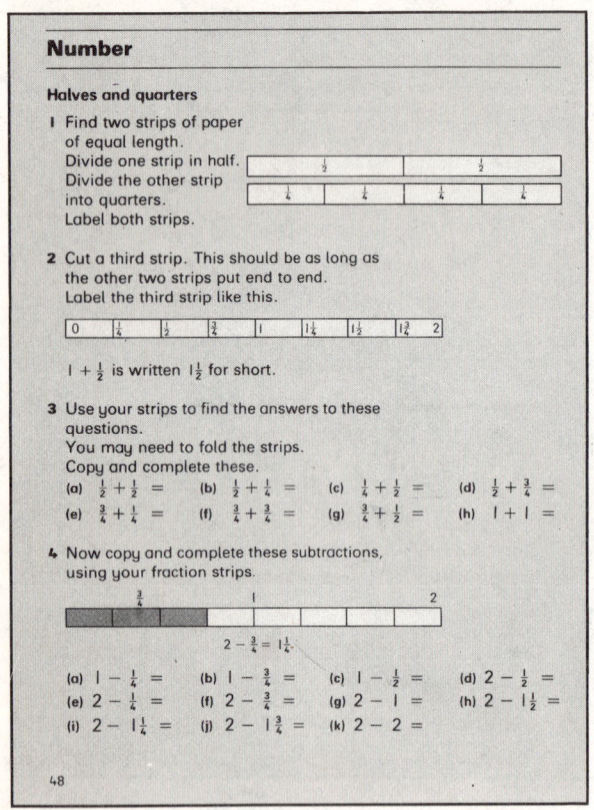

Number

Halves and quarters

1. Find two strips of paper of equal length.
   Divide one strip in half.
   Divide the other strip into quarters.
   Label both strips.

2. Cut a third strip. This should be as long as the other two strips put end to end.
   Label the third strip like this.

   $1 + \frac{1}{2}$ is written $1\frac{1}{2}$ for short.

3. Use your strips to find the answers to these questions.
   You may need to fold the strips.
   Copy and complete these.
   (a) $\frac{1}{2} + \frac{1}{2} =$ (b) $\frac{1}{2} + \frac{1}{4} =$ (c) $\frac{1}{4} + \frac{1}{2} =$ (d) $\frac{1}{2} + \frac{3}{4} =$
   (e) $\frac{3}{4} + \frac{1}{4} =$ (f) $\frac{1}{4} + \frac{3}{4} =$ (g) $\frac{3}{4} + \frac{1}{2} =$ (h) $1 + 1 =$

4. Now copy and complete these subtractions, using your fraction strips.

   $2 - \frac{3}{4} = 1\frac{1}{4}$

   (a) $1 - \frac{1}{4} =$ (b) $1 - \frac{3}{4} =$ (c) $1 - \frac{1}{2} =$ (d) $2 - \frac{1}{2} =$
   (e) $2 - \frac{1}{4} =$ (f) $2 - \frac{3}{4} =$ (g) $2 - 1 =$ (h) $2 - 1\frac{1}{2} =$
   (i) $2 - 1\frac{1}{4} =$ (j) $2 - 1\frac{3}{4} =$ (k) $2 - 2 =$

48

Content
Consolidation of addition and subtraction of simple fractions. Extension to fractions greater than 1.

Equipment
paper strips

Notes
1. Check that the three strips are the same length and are labelled correctly.

Q3 (a) 1 (b) $\frac{3}{4}$ (c) $\frac{3}{4}$ (d) $1\frac{1}{4}$ (e) 1 (f) $1\frac{1}{2}$
    (g) $1\frac{1}{4}$ (h) 2

Q4 (a) $\frac{3}{4}$ (b) $\frac{1}{4}$ (c) $\frac{1}{2}$ (d) $1\frac{1}{2}$ (e) $1\frac{3}{4}$ (f) $1\frac{1}{4}$
    (g) 1 (h) $\frac{1}{2}$ (i) $\frac{3}{4}$ (j) $\frac{1}{4}$ (k) 0

Worksheet 11 gives more practice with fractions and money.

Answers
1 15, $\frac{3}{4}$ **2** 25, $\frac{1}{2}$ **3** 9, 27, $\frac{3}{4}$ **4** 25, $\frac{1}{4}$, $\frac{3}{4}$

Page 49 Fifths and tenths

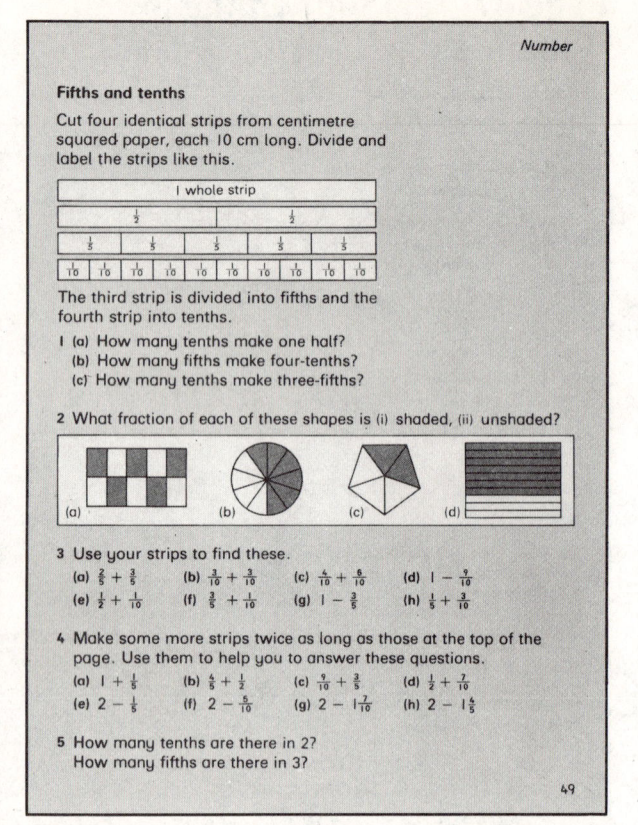

Number

Fifths and tenths

Cut four identical strips from centimetre squared paper, each 10 cm long. Divide and label the strips like this.

The third strip is divided into fifths and the fourth strip into tenths.

1. (a) How many tenths make one half?
   (b) How many fifths make four-tenths?
   (c) How many tenths make three-fifths?

2. What fraction of each of these shapes is (i) shaded, (ii) unshaded?

   (a)   (b)   (c)   (d)

3. Use your strips to find these.
   (a) $\frac{2}{5} + \frac{3}{5}$ (b) $\frac{3}{10} + \frac{3}{10}$ (c) $\frac{4}{10} + \frac{6}{10}$ (d) $1 - \frac{9}{10}$
   (e) $\frac{1}{2} + \frac{1}{10}$ (f) $\frac{3}{5} + \frac{1}{10}$ (g) $1 - \frac{3}{5}$ (h) $\frac{1}{5} + \frac{3}{10}$

4. Make some more strips twice as long as those at the top of the page. Use them to help you to answer these questions.
   (a) $1 + \frac{1}{5}$ (b) $\frac{4}{5} + \frac{1}{2}$ (c) $\frac{9}{10} + \frac{3}{5}$ (d) $\frac{1}{2} + \frac{7}{10}$
   (e) $2 - \frac{1}{5}$ (f) $2 - \frac{5}{10}$ (g) $2 - 1\frac{7}{10}$ (h) $2 - 1\frac{4}{5}$

5. How many tenths are there in 2?
   How many fifths are there in 3?

49

Content
Finding equivalent fractions, using paper strips, for $\frac{1}{5}$ and $\frac{1}{10}$; adding and subtracting fractions.

Vocabulary
fifth, tenth

Equipment
paper strips

Notes
1. Check that the strips are divided and labelled correctly before they are used to answer questions.

Q1 (a) 5 (b) 2 (c) 6

Q2 (a) (i) $\frac{1}{2}$ or $\frac{5}{10}$ (ii) $\frac{1}{2}$ or $\frac{5}{10}$ $\frac{6}{10}$
    (b) (i) $\frac{3}{5}$ or $\frac{6}{10}$ (ii) $\frac{2}{5}$ or $\frac{4}{10}$
    (c) (i) $\frac{2}{5}$ (ii) $\frac{3}{5}$ *Not in all versions*
    (d) (i) $\frac{7}{10}$ (ii) $\frac{3}{10}$

Q3 (a) 1 or $\frac{5}{5}$ (b) $\frac{3}{5}$ or $\frac{6}{10}$ (c) 1 or $\frac{10}{10}$
    (d) $\frac{1}{10}$ (e) $\frac{3}{5}$ or $\frac{6}{10}$ (f) $\frac{7}{10}$ (g) $\frac{2}{5}$
    (h) $\frac{1}{2}$ or $\frac{5}{10}$

28

Q4 (a) $1\frac{1}{5}$ or $\frac{6}{5}$ (b) $1\frac{3}{10}$ or $\frac{13}{10}$
(c) $1\frac{1}{2}$ or $1\frac{5}{10}$ or $\frac{15}{10}$
(d) $1\frac{1}{5}$ or $1\frac{2}{10}$ or $\frac{12}{10}$ or $\frac{6}{5}$
(e) $1\frac{4}{5}$ or $\frac{9}{5}$
(f) $1\frac{1}{2}$ or $1\frac{5}{10}$ or $\frac{15}{10}$ (g) $\frac{3}{10}$ (h) $\frac{1}{5}$

Q5 20, 15

Pages 50 and 51 Practise your subtraction

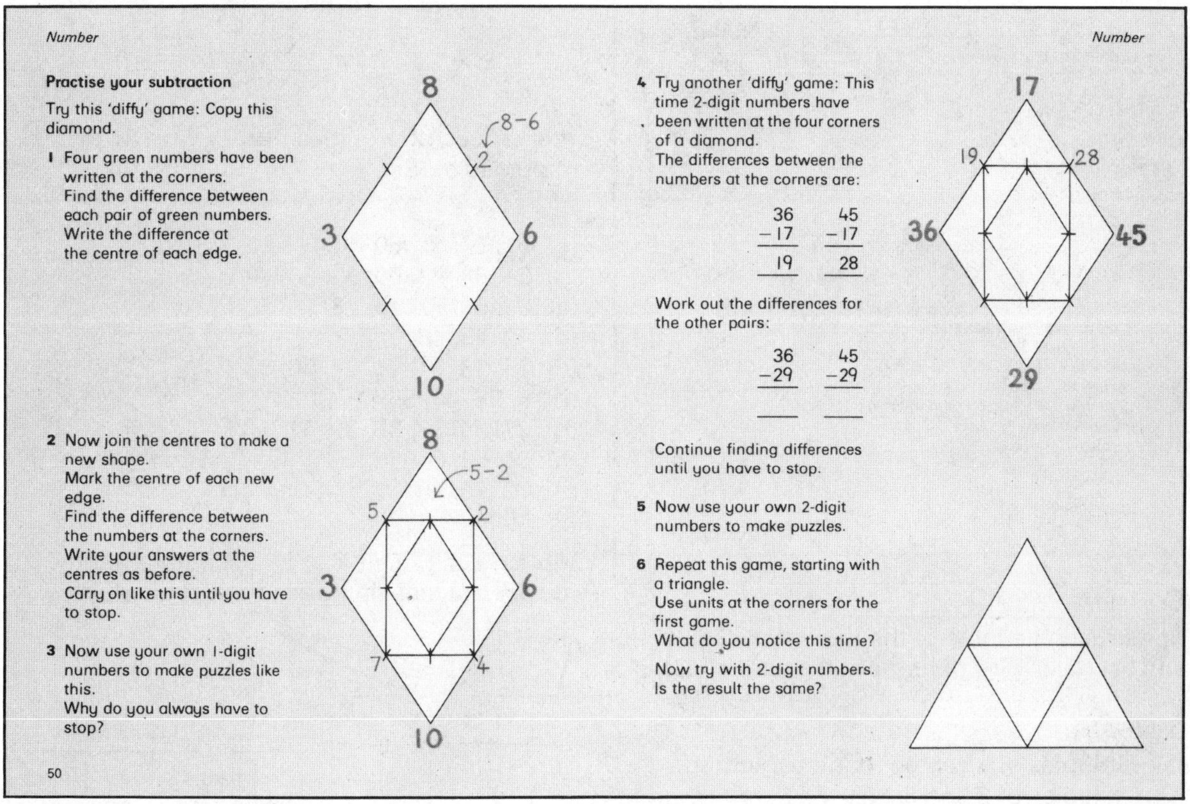

Content
The diffy game played (a) with four 1-digit numbers; (b) with four 2-digit numbers; (c) using a triangle for the numbers.

Equipment
number line

Notes
1. Make sure that the first shape is large enough to contain the subsequent shapes — use a whole page.
2. The example on page 50 stops after the fourth set of subtractions because the answers are all 0.
3. Give the children opportunities to experiment. With this shape, 0 will always be reached. Each time, ask the children to count the number of shapes (the number of subtractions). Ask them if they can find numbers which will require more than seven subtractions to reach 0.
4. Some children may need a number line to calculate the differences on page 51.
5. For quadrilaterals, 0 is always reached.

Q5 With the triangle 1, 1, 0 is eventually reached. The children may notice after the first subtraction that the numbers form an addition (or subtraction) trio; eg $2 + 5 = 7$, $7 - 5 = 2$.

6. *Extend* this work with other shapes, eg pentagon, hexagon.

Page 52 Looking at multiples

Number

Looking at multiples

1 Make a table to record the multiples of 3, the multiples of 6 and the multiples of 9.

×	1	2	3	4	5	6	7	8	9	10
3	3	6	9							
6	6	12	18							
9	9	18	27							

2 Look at the multiples of 3.
$3 \times 4 = 12$ Add the digits, $1 + 2 = 3$.
$3 \times 5 = 15$ Add the digits, $1 + 5 = 6$.
Continue doing this.
What do you notice?

3 Do the same with the multiples of 6.
What do you notice?

4 Now add the digits of the multiples of 9. Do all the digits of all multiples of 9 add to the single digit 9?
Look at $9 \times 11 = 99$. Add the digits, $9 + 9 = 18$. Add again, $1 + 8 = 9$.
Try multiples of 9 greater than 100. Is the digit sum always 9?

Content

Constructing a table of the multiples of 3, 6, and 9. Looking for patterns in the sum of digits.

Notes

Q1 Multiples of 9 can be found by adding multiples of 3 and 6.

Q2 The sums of the digits for multiples of 3 are always 3, 6, 9.

Q3 The sums of the digits for multiples of 6 are always 6, 3, 9 eg $48 \rightarrow 12 \rightarrow 3$.

Q4 All the multiples of 9 in the chart give a digit sum of 9. Notice how the numbers are reversals, eg 18 and 81, 27 and 72. Multiples of 9 greater than 100 still give a digit sum of 9,
eg $9 \times 13 = 117$; $1 + 1 + 7 \longrightarrow 9$
$9 \times 24 = 216$; $2 + 1 + 6 \longrightarrow 9$.

Worksheet 12 provides further work with multiples of 3.

Answers
(a) 51, 54, 57, 60
(b) 81, 84, 87, 90, 93, 96, 99
(c) 66, 69, 72, 75, 78
(d) 42, 45, 48
(e) 15, 18, 21, 24, 27, 30, 33
(f) 6, 36, 66, 96
(g) 27, 30, 33, 36, 39, 42
(h) 24, 54, 84
(i) 72, 75, 78
(j) 102

Worksheet 13 can also be used here to give further practice, in puzzle form, of multiples.

Answers
1

−	30	28	26	24
9	21	19	17	15
7	23	21	19	17
5	25	23	21	19
3	27	25	23	21
1	29	27	25	23

−	41	43	45	47	49
8	33	35	37	39	41
6	35	37	39	41	43
4	37	39	41	43	45
2	39	41	43	45	47

2 A boat. Multiples of 3.
3 A face. Multiples of 6.

Page 53 More nines

> **More nines**
>
> | × | 10 | 11 | 12 | 13 | 14 | 15 | 16 | 17 | 18 | 19 | 20 |
> |---|---|---|---|---|---|---|---|---|---|---|---|
> | 9 | | | | | | | | | | | |
> | Sum of digits | | | | | | | | | | | |
> | Sum as a single digit | | | | | | | | | | | |
>
> 1 Fill in the table showing multiples of 9. When you do not know the answer, you can use this method to find out.
>
> 12×9 $\quad$ $\begin{array}{r} 10 + 2 \\ \times\ 9 \\ \hline 90 + 18 \end{array} \rightarrow 108$ $\quad$ or $\quad \begin{array}{r} 12 \\ \times\ 9 \\ \hline 108 \end{array}$
>
> What do you notice about the digit sum of all the multiples of 9?
>
> 2 Add the digits of these telephone numbers to see whether the numbers are multiples of 9.
> 3033   2718   3602   1629   2217   8145
> Is your telephone number a multiple of 9?
>
> 3 Collect the telephone numbers of your friends.
> Find the digit sums.
> How many are multiples of 9? How many are not multiples of 9?

Content
Building up a table of the multiples of 9 from 10 to 20 and finding the sum of the digits.

Notes
1. Check that the first line filled in on the chart is correct.
2. Remind children how to find the digit sum as a single digit.

×	10	11	12	13	14	15	16	17	18	19	20
9	90	99	108	117	126	135	144	153	162	171	180
Sum of digits	9	18	9	9	9	9	9	9	9	9	9
Sum as a single digit	9	9	9	9	9	9	9	9	9	9	9

3. The children should notice that the digit sum of all the multiples of 9 is 9.
   3033, 2718, 1629, 8145 are all multiples of 9.
4. The results of the telephone survey could be displayed as a graph.

Volume and capacity

Pages 54 and 55 Introducing volume and capacity

Content
Finding whether the children can (a) halve a litre of water; (b) find an amount of water of the same volume as a rock; (c) find a pile of stones of the same volume as the rock.

Vocabulary
litre

Equipment
litre measure, plastic bottles (1 litre), identical containers of about $\frac{1}{2}$-litre capacity, other containers which hold $\frac{1}{2}$-litre or more, rocks, containers which will hold the rocks snugly, string, plastic bags

Notes

1. Check that the children mark the litre level on the bottle (plastic lemonade bottles could be used).

2. The plastic bags should be transparent but tough, and large enough to hold the containers. Check that the children lower the rock gently into the water, leaving the free end of the string over the jug.

Q3 The water in the bag should have the same volume as the stone. The children can make a rough check by pushing the bag of water into the shape of the rock.

Q4 Most children will think of putting the estimated pile of stones into the container of water from which the rock has been removed. Ask them, 'Does the water level now reach the brim? Did the water overflow? Was your estimate too high or too low?'

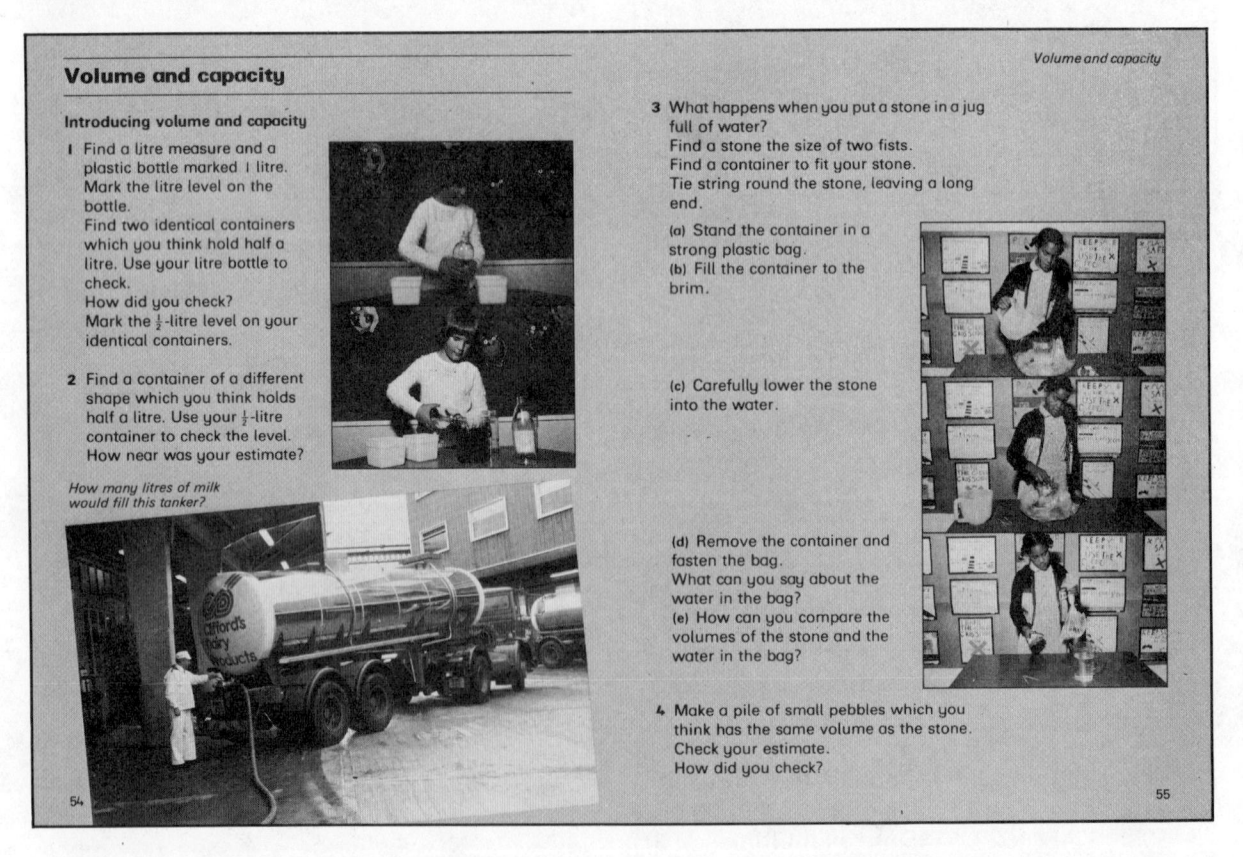

Volume and capacity

Introducing volume and capacity

1. Find a litre measure and a plastic bottle marked 1 litre. Mark the litre level on the bottle.
Find two identical containers which you think hold half a litre. Use your litre bottle to check.
How did you check?
Mark the $\frac{1}{2}$-litre level on your identical containers.

2. Find a container of a different shape which you think holds half a litre. Use your $\frac{1}{2}$-litre container to check the level.
How near was your estimate?

How many litres of milk would fill this tanker?

3. What happens when you put a stone in a jug full of water?
Find a stone the size of two fists.
Find a container to fit your stone.
Tie string round the stone, leaving a long end.

(a) Stand the container in a strong plastic bag.
(b) Fill the container to the brim.

(c) Carefully lower the stone into the water.

(d) Remove the container and fasten the bag.
What can you say about the water in the bag?
(e) How can you compare the volumes of the stone and the water in the bag?

4. Make a pile of small pebbles which you think has the same volume as the stone.
Check your estimate.
How did you check?

Pages 56 and 57 The school garden

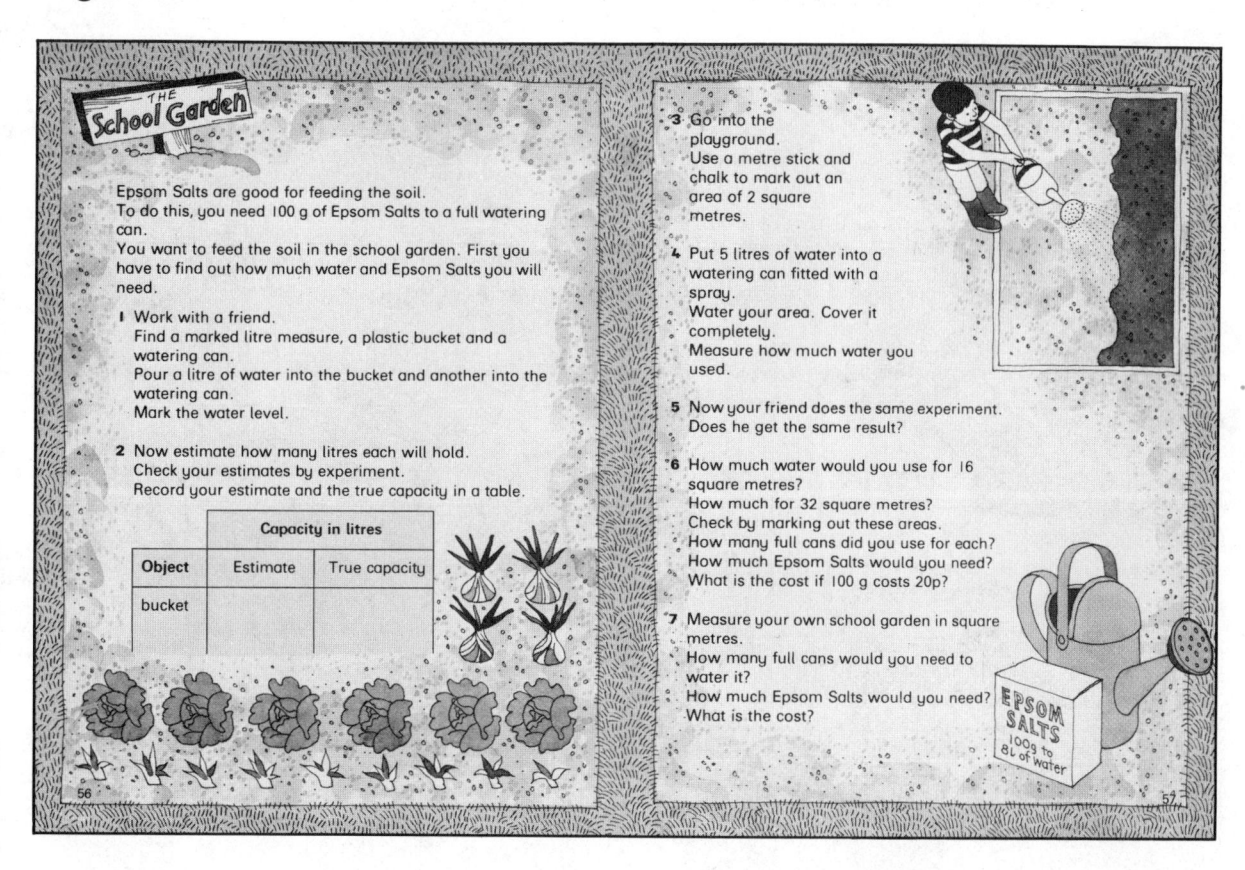

> ## The School Garden
>
> Epsom Salts are good for feeding the soil.
> To do this, you need 100 g of Epsom Salts to a full watering can.
> You want to feed the soil in the school garden. First you have to find out how much water and Epsom Salts you will need.
>
> 1. Work with a friend.
>   Find a marked litre measure, a plastic bucket and a watering can.
>   Pour a litre of water into the bucket and another into the watering can.
>   Mark the water level.
>
> 2. Now estimate how many litres each will hold.
>   Check your estimates by experiment.
>   Record your estimate and the true capacity in a table.
>
> | Object | Capacity in litres ||
> |--------|----------|---------------|
> | | Estimate | True capacity |
> | bucket | | |
>
> 3. Go into the playground.
>   Use a metre stick and chalk to mark out an area of 2 square metres.
>
> 4. Put 5 litres of water into a watering can fitted with a spray.
>   Water your area. Cover it completely.
>   Measure how much water you used.
>
> 5. Now your friend does the same experiment. Does he get the same result?
>
> 6. How much water would you use for 16 square metres?
>   How much for 32 square metres?
>   Check by marking out these areas.
>   How many full cans did you use for each?
>   How much Epsom Salts would you need?
>   What is the cost if 100 g costs 20p?
>
> 7. Measure your own school garden in square metres.
>   How many full cans would you need to water it?
>   How much Epsom Salts would you need?
>   What is the cost?
>
> *Epsom Salts 100g to 8L of water*

Content
Finding the capacity, in litres, of buckets and watering cans. Finding the volume of water used on the school garden.

Vocabulary
square metre

Equipment
watering can with spray, bucket, litre measures, metre sticks, chalk

Notes

1. Precede by discussing estimation. An estimate is not a wild guess. It should be as near as you can get. For example, when estimating how many litres a watering can or bucket will hold, ask the children to show where they think the water level would be for 1 litre. Let them check and correct the water level. This new level will help them to make a better estimate of the capacity of the bucket or watering can.

2. Watering cans and buckets usually hold 8 or 9 litres of water.

3. To spray 2 square metres completely, children will probably use between 2 and 4 litres.

4. Ask the children to find how much water is needed for 5 square metres, etc.

5. *Extend* by asking the children to find the area they could water with a full can (8 litres). They will find this easier if they first draw metre squares to cover part of the playground and water the marked section.

Pages 58 and 59 Introducing millilitres

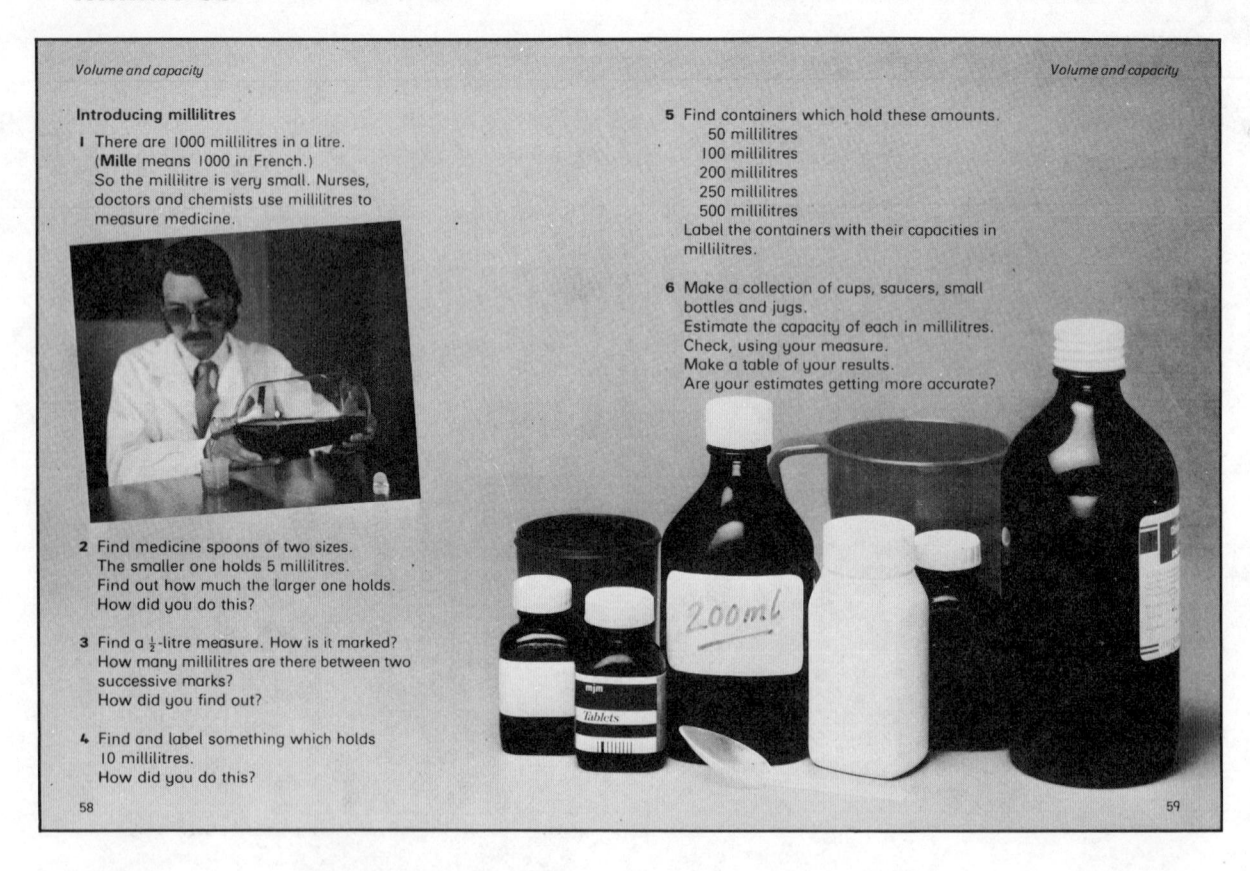

Volume and capacity

Introducing millilitres

1. There are 1000 millilitres in a litre.
   (**Mille** means 1000 in French.)
   So the millilitre is very small. Nurses, doctors and chemists use millilitres to measure medicine.

2. Find medicine spoons of two sizes.
   The smaller one holds 5 millilitres.
   Find out how much the larger one holds.
   How did you do this?

3. Find a ½-litre measure. How is it marked?
   How many millilitres are there between two successive marks?
   How did you find out?

4. Find and label something which holds 10 millilitres.
   How did you do this?

5. Find containers which hold these amounts.
   50 millilitres
   100 millilitres
   200 millilitres
   250 millilitres
   500 millilitres
   Label the containers with their capacities in millilitres.

6. Make a collection of cups, saucers, small bottles and jugs.
   Estimate the capacity of each in millilitres.
   Check, using your measure.
   Make a table of your results.
   Are your estimates getting more accurate?

Content
Introducing the millilitre (ml). Familiarising the children with containers of 5 millilitres to 500 millilitres in capacity. Estimating the capacities of various domestic containers using a graduated measure.

Vocabulary
millilitre (ml), graduated, graduations, successive

Equipment
medicine spoons (5 ml and 10 ml), litre or ½-litre measure, containers of capacities 50 ml, 100 ml, 200 ml, 250 ml, 500 ml, unbreakable cups, saucers, mugs, jugs

Notes

1. Plastic medicine spoons are obtainable from chemist shops. Suitable plastic containers would be shampoo bottles and other bottles from the chemist. Ask the children to bring these.

2. It is useful for children (a) to recognise containers of 100 ml capacity; (b) to know the approximate capacities of familiar objects such as cups and saucers

3. All the containers used should be labelled with their approximate capacities. Question the children from time to time about these capacities.

Q4 Bottle caps often have a capacity of 10 ml.

Area

Page 60 Making squares and rectangles

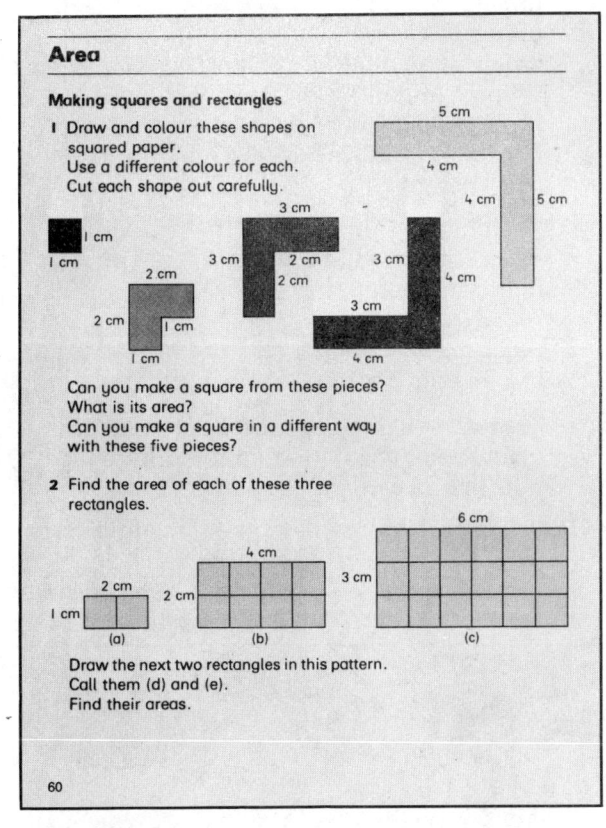

> ### Area
>
> **Making squares and rectangles**
>
> 1 Draw and colour these shapes on squared paper.
> Use a different colour for each.
> Cut each shape out carefully.
>
> Can you make a square from these pieces?
> What is its area?
> Can you make a square in a different way with these five pieces?
>
> 2 Find the area of each of these three rectangles.
>
> Draw the next two rectangles in this pattern.
> Call them (d) and (e).
> Find their areas.

Content
Finding areas of squares and rectangles in square centimetres.

Equipment
centimetre squared paper (or 2-centimetre squared paper, if preferred), scissors, coloured pencils

Notes
1. If 2 centimetre squared paper is used, the area can be given as the number of squares.
2. The square in Q1 can be made in two ways using all the pieces: as on page 15, with the square centimetre in one corner, or as a spiral with the square centimetre in the middle.
3. Ask the children to find the ratio of the edges of each rectangle they draw.
(d) 32 sq cm   (e) 50 sq cm.
4. *Extend* by asking the children to make each rectangle in a different colour. The rectangles can be placed one on top of the other, starting at one corner, as on page 15. Ask the children what they notice about the opposite corners of the pattern of rectangles (they are in a straight line). This happens because all these rectangles are the same shape. The ratio of their edges is the same.

Page 61 Find the rectangles

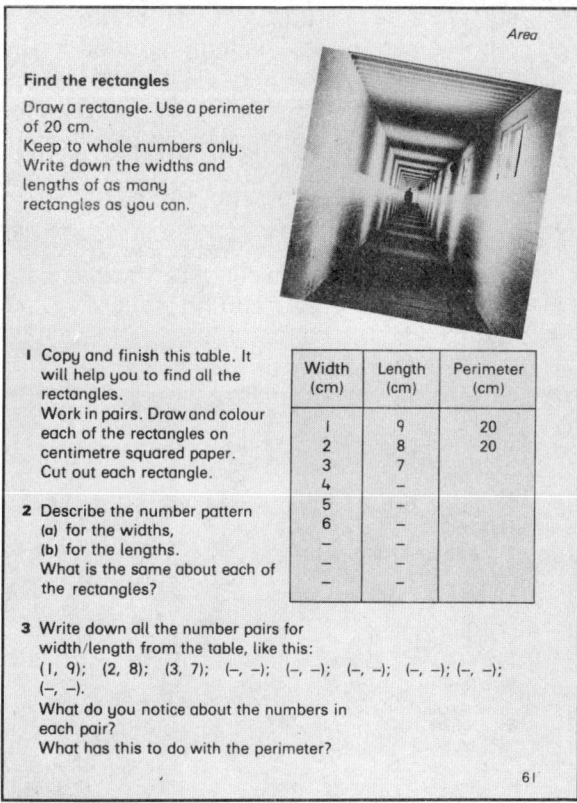

> **Find the rectangles**
>
> Draw a rectangle. Use a perimeter of 20 cm.
> Keep to whole numbers only.
> Write down the widths and lengths of as many rectangles as you can.
>
> 1 Copy and finish this table. It will help you to find all the rectangles.
> Work in pairs. Draw and colour each of the rectangles on centimetre squared paper.
> Cut out each rectangle.
>
> | Width (cm) | Length (cm) | Perimeter (cm) |
> |---|---|---|
> | 1 | 9 | 20 |
> | 2 | 8 | 20 |
> | 3 | 7 | |
> | 4 | – | |
> | 5 | – | |
> | 6 | – | |
> | – | – | |
> | – | – | |
>
> 2 Describe the number pattern
> (a) for the widths,
> (b) for the lengths.
> What is the same about each of the rectangles?
>
> 3 Write down all the number pairs for width/length from the table, like this:
> (1, 9); (2, 8); (3, 7); (–, –); (–, –); (–, –); (–, –); (–, –); (–, –).
> What do you notice about the numbers in each pair?
> What has this to do with the perimeter?

Content
Finding the dimensions and number patterns of all possible rectangles with the same perimeter (using whole numbers only).

Vocabulary
increase, decrease

Equipment
centimetre squared paper, coloured pencils, scissors

Notes

1. When describing the patterns of the width and lengths, introduce the correct vocabulary: 'The width increases by 1 each time (starting at 1, finishing at 9)'. 'The length decreases by 1 each time'.

2. Some children may be able to suggest a rectangle 10 centimetres long and zero centimetres wide. This is more likely if the children make their rectangles using a narrow paper strip 20 centimetres long, marked in centimetres, and joined end-to-end.

Q3 The perimeters of the rectangles are all the same: 20 centimetres. The numbers in each pair have sum 10. 10 centimetres is half the perimeter. The length added to the width is half the perimeter – 10 centimetres.

Pages 62 and 63 Rectangle patterns

Content

Calculating the areas of sets of rectangles with the same perimeters. Arranging a set of rectangles with the same perimeters in a mathematical pattern.

Equipment

centimetre squared paper, scissors, coloured pencils, string

Notes

Q1 The square has the largest area. (Squares belong to the set of rectangles but not to the set of oblongs, which must have their edges of different lengths – *ob*). The smallest area in the table is 9 sq cm. The difference pattern of successive areas in the table is a set of decreasing odd numbers. After the square, the odd numbers increase.

Q2 The children will arrange the rectangle in different ways but the areas must be kept in order. See opposite.

Ask the children what is the same about all the rectangles. How are they different?

Extend by using other perimeters to give further practice in finding the difference number patterns.

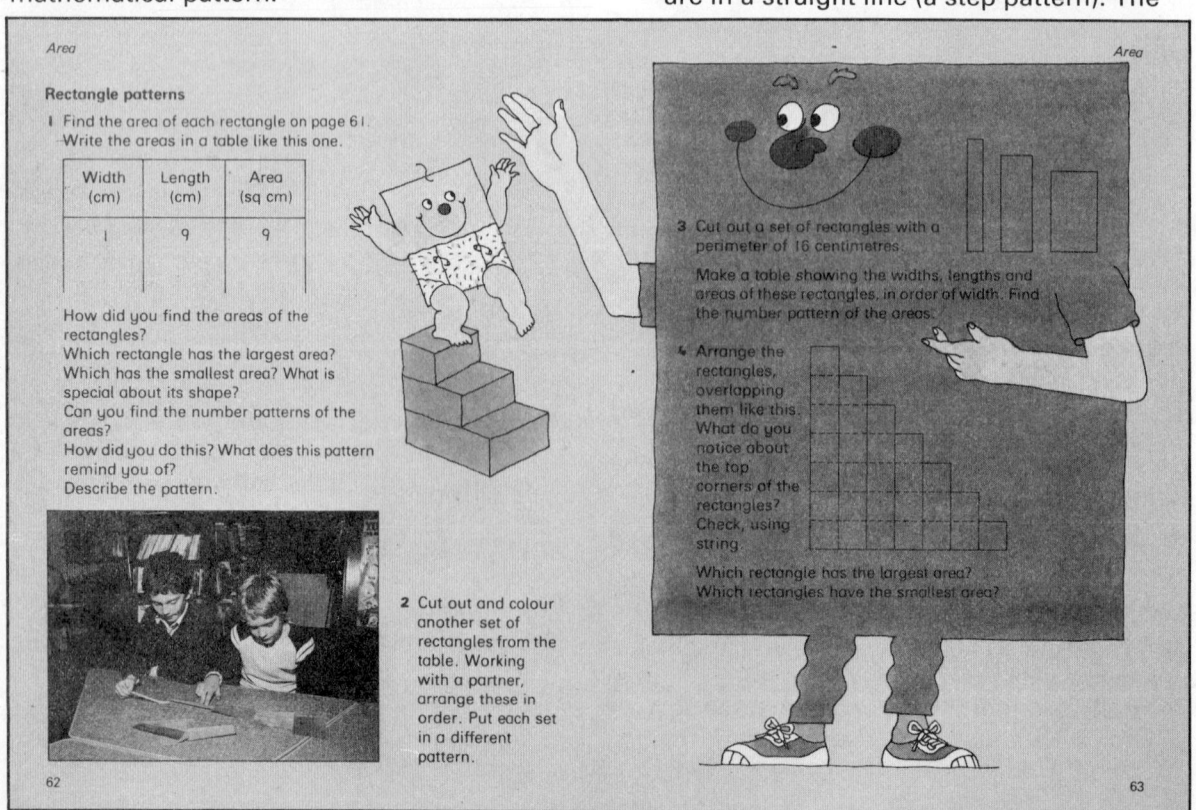

Q3 In this arrangement, all the rectangles start from the same corner and have two common edges. The top right-hand corners are in a straight line (a step pattern). The

rectangle with the largest area is the 4 cm by 4 cm square. Two rectangles have the smallest area (7 sq cm).

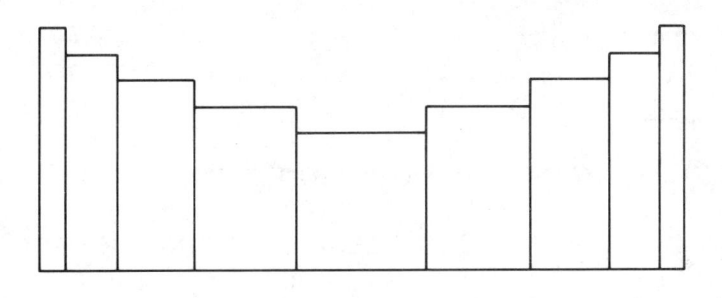

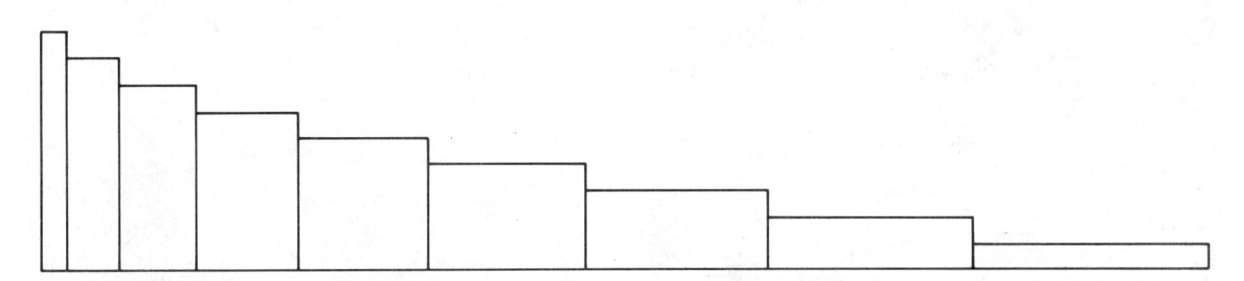

The pattern of the areas in the table is obtained by subtracting one area from the next. Encourage the children to look for the pattern themselves before asking them to find the 'difference' pattern. Once more, the areas form a decreasing sequence of odd numbers (then increasing).

Extend by providing other perimeters (multiples of 4).

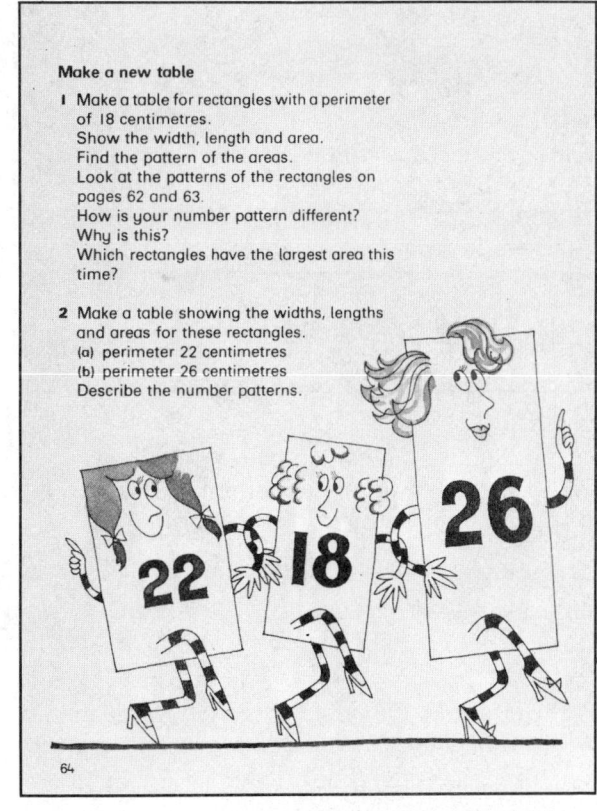

Page 64 Make a new table

Content
Making and using a table showing the width, length and area of rectangles when half perimeters are an odd number of centimetres.

Equipment
centimetre squared paper, scissors

Notes
1. Some children will need to cut out the rectangles with a perimeter of 18 cm.

2. When half the perimeter is an odd number of centimetres, the area of the rectangle will always be an even number of square centimetres. If the children do not notice this, ask them to compare the tables for the rectangles on pages 63 and 64. All the rectangles on page 64 have areas which are an even number of square centimetres. Some children may notice that there is no longer one rectangle (a square) with largest area, but two. Ask them if they can find a square with area larger than these two rectangles.

Make a new table

1 Make a table for rectangles with a perimeter of 18 centimetres.
Show the width, length and area.
Find the pattern of the areas.
Look at the patterns of the rectangles on pages 62 and 63.
How is your number pattern different?
Why is this?
Which rectangles have the largest area this time?

2 Make a table showing the widths, lengths and areas for these rectangles.
(a) perimeter 22 centimetres
(b) perimeter 26 centimetres
Describe the number patterns.

37

Number

Q1 132 Q2 72 Q3 52 Q4 112 Q5 115
Q6 87 Q7 54 Q8 138 Q9 308 Q10 126
Q11 215 Q12 424 Q13 (a) 144 (b) 288

Page 65 How much chocolate?

Page 66 A division game

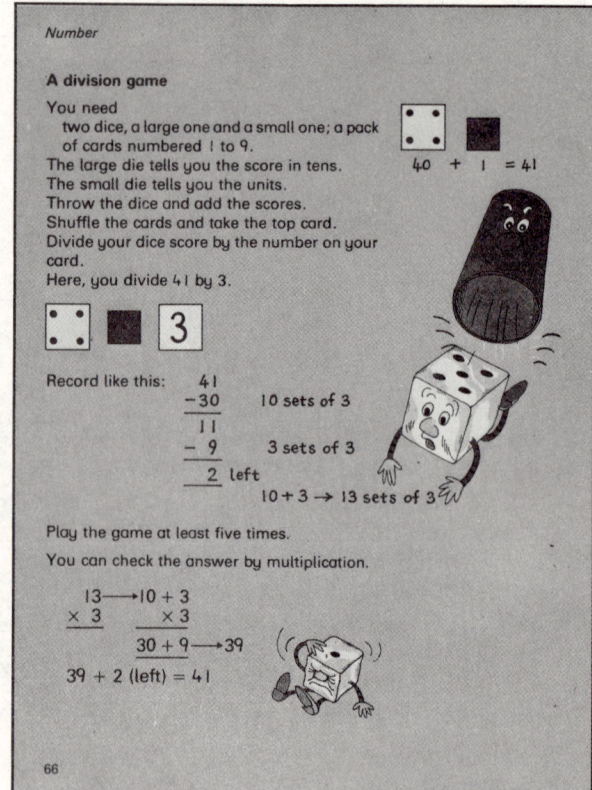

Content

Extending multiplication by (a) drawing on squared paper, (b) expanded form. Practice and problems using multiplication.

Equipment

squared paper

Notes

1. Squared paper will be needed for each multiplication.

2. Check that each child understands that $5 \times 10 = 50$ and $5 \times 20 = 100$ from the diagram. It is worth spending time multiplying single digits by 10, 20, etc to build up confidence.

3. Show that the expanded form of multiplying gives the same result as drawing and counting squares.

Content

Dividing numbers from 11 to 66 by a single-digit number. Checking by multiplication.

Equipment

dice, cards numbered 1 to 9, ten-sticks and units

Notes

1. Precede by checking that children can multiply single-digit numbers by 10.

2. Encourage the children to subtract the largest obvious group, eg groups of 10 or 5.

3. Encourage the children to check the answers by multiplication. Some children should continue until all the cards have been used.

4. *Extend* by asking the children to find the largest and smallest answers that can be

obtained in this game (66 ÷ 1 and 11 ÷ 9). Ask them what the highest possible remainder would be.

Page 67 A remainder game

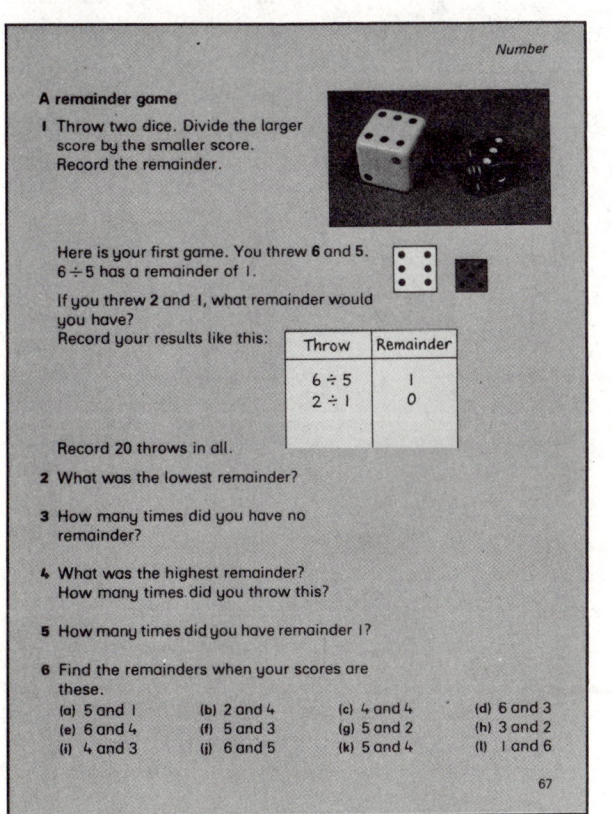

> Number
>
> **A remainder game**
> 1 Throw two dice. Divide the larger score by the smaller score. Record the remainder.
>
> Here is your first game. You threw **6** and **5**.
> 6 ÷ 5 has a remainder of 1.
>
> If you threw **2** and **1**, what remainder would you have?
> Record your results like this:
>
> | Throw | Remainder |
> |---|---|
> | 6 ÷ 5 | 1 |
> | 2 ÷ 1 | 0 |
>
> Record 20 throws in all.
>
> 2 What was the lowest remainder?
>
> 3 How many times did you have no remainder?
>
> 4 What was the highest remainder? How many times did you throw this?
>
> 5 How many times did you have remainder 1?
>
> 6 Find the remainders when your scores are these.
> (a) 5 and 1 (b) 2 and 4 (c) 4 and 4 (d) 6 and 3
> (e) 6 and 4 (f) 5 and 3 (g) 5 and 2 (h) 3 and 2
> (i) 4 and 3 (j) 6 and 5 (k) 5 and 4 (l) 1 and 6
>
> 67

Content
Finding the remainders when two dice are thrown and the higher score is divided by the lower score. Looking for patterns.

Equipment
dice, counters

Notes
1. Make sure that the children understand that they are recording remainders only.
2. Some children will need counters to find the remainders.
3. The lowest remainder is 0. The highest remainder is 2.
4. Check that the children always divide the larger score by the smaller score.
5. There is some value in collecting together more than 20 scores and looking at the remainder pattern produced. The following table shows how the remainders occur.

		\multicolumn{6}{c}{First die}
		1	2	3	4	5	6
	1	0	0	0	0	0	0
	2	0	0	1	0	1	0
Second	3	0	1	0	1	2	0
die	4	0	0	1	0	1	2
	5	0	1	2	1	0	1
	6	0	0	0	2	1	0

Remember to divide the larger score by the smaller.
22 possible remainders of 0 out of 36.
10 possible remainders of 1 out of 36.
4 possible remainders of 2 out of 36.

Q6 (a) 0 (b) 0 (c) 0 (d) 0 (e) 2 (f) 2
    (g) 1 (h) 1 (i) 1 (j) 1 (k) 1 (l) 0

Pages 68 and 69 Square sequences

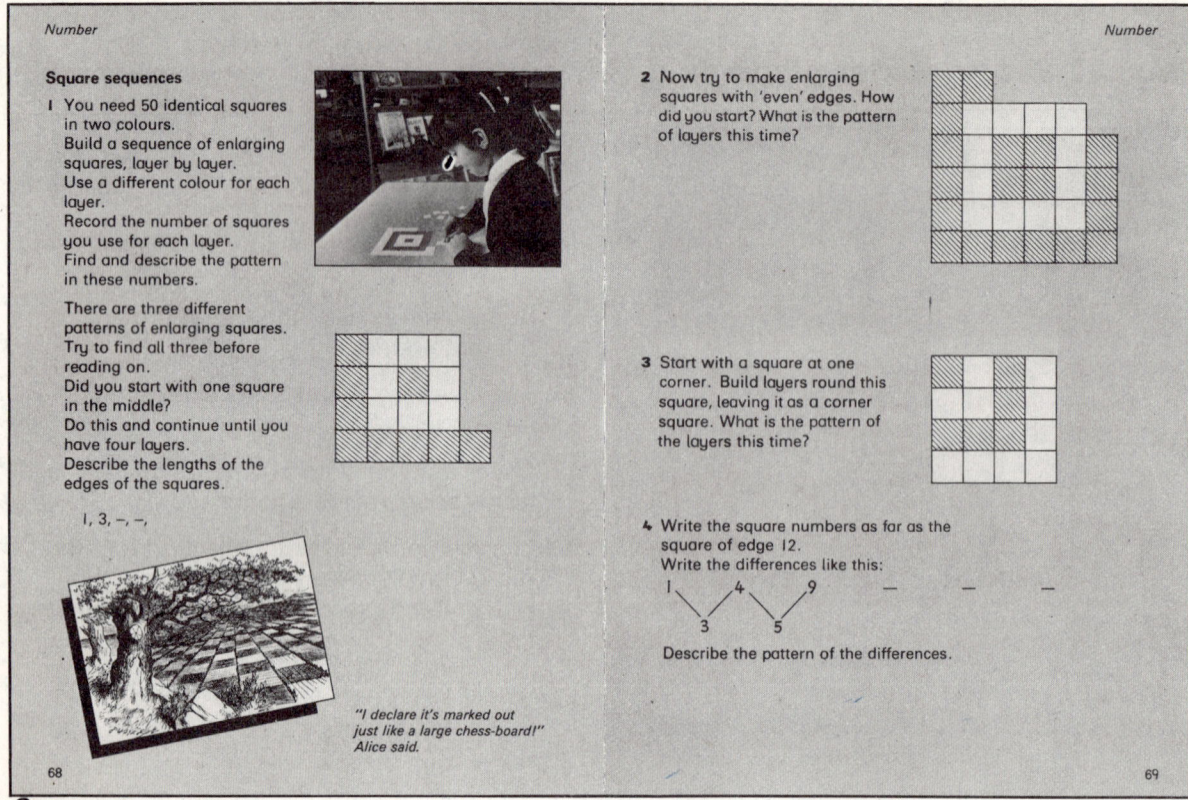

Number

Square sequences

1. You need 50 identical squares in two colours.
   Build a sequence of enlarging squares, layer by layer.
   Use a different colour for each layer.
   Record the number of squares you use for each layer.
   Find and describe the pattern in these numbers.

   There are three different patterns of enlarging squares. Try to find all three before reading on.
   Did you start with one square in the middle?
   Do this and continue until you have four layers.
   Describe the lengths of the edges of the squares.

   1, 3, –, –,

   "I declare it's marked out just like a large chess-board!" Alice said.

2. Now try to make enlarging squares with 'even' edges. How did you start? What is the pattern of layers this time?

3. Start with a square at one corner. Build layers round this square, leaving it as a corner square. What is the pattern of the layers this time?

4. Write the square numbers as far as the square of edge 12.
   Write the differences like this:

   1   4   9   —   —   —
     3   5

   Describe the pattern of the differences.

Content
Building sequences of squares using identical unit squares. Describing the patterns.

Vocabulary
enlarging, layer

Equipment
identical squares in two colours

Notes

1. The order in which children build their square patterns will vary – see illustrations on pages 68 and 69.

Q1 Layers: 1, 8, 16, 24. Ask the children, in pairs, to estimate and check the next layer. Ask them, 'How many units did you use altogether?' (81 units)

Q2 Layers: 4, 12, 20, 28. Repeat questions as in Q1. The children should check using unit squares.

Q3 Layers: 1, 3, 5, 7. Repeat questions as in Q1.

Q4 The square numbers are 1, 4, 9, 16, 25, 36, 49, 64, 81, 100, 121, 144.
There is an odd-number difference pattern. The differences are the set of odd numbers 3, 5, 7, 9.

Page 70 What can you buy?

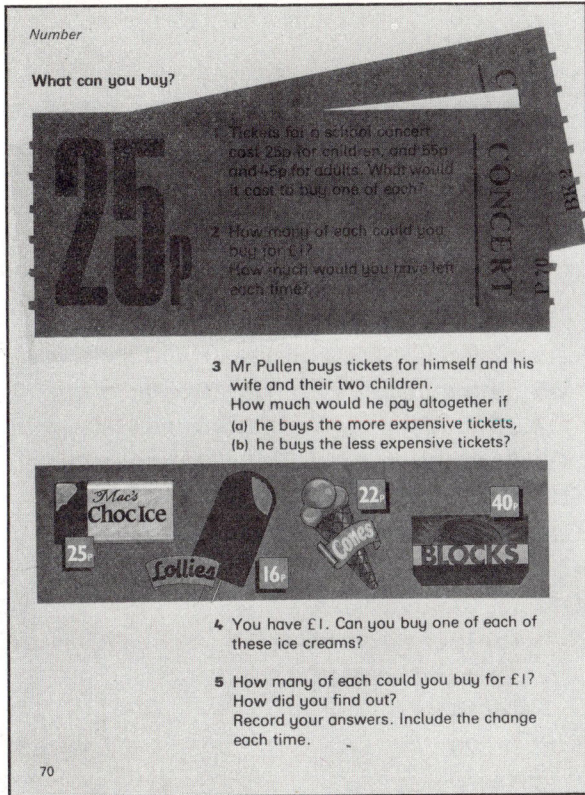

Content
Using the four operations to solve money problems.

Notes

Q1 £1.25 (125p)

Q2 Four at 25p, one at 55p, two at 45p. Change would be 0p, 45p, and 10p.

Q3 (a) £1.60 (160p)   (b) £1.40 (140p)

Q4 No. You would need 3p more.

Q5 4 at 25p, 6 at 16p, 4 at 22p, 2 at 40p. Change would be 0p, 4p, 12p, 20p.

1. *Extend* this work by letting the children make up similar problems based on local prices.

Page 71 Party time

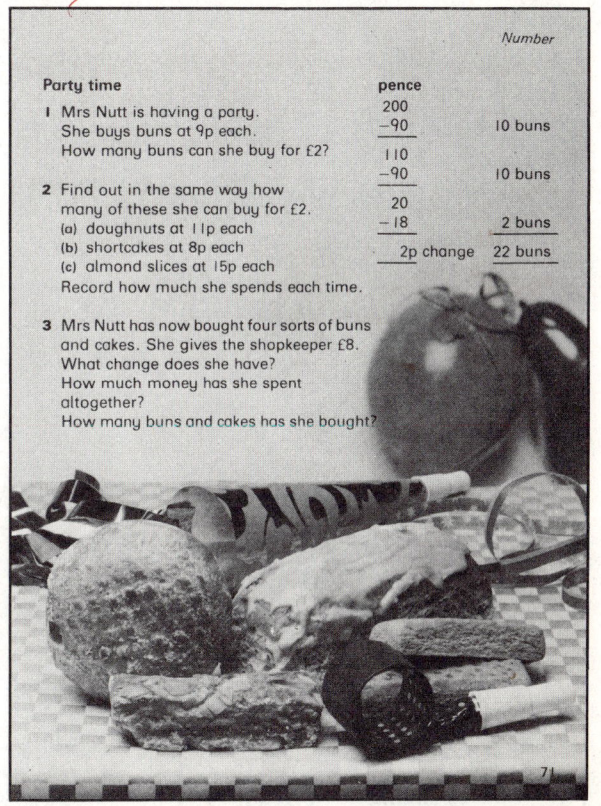

Content
Division of larger amounts of money using repeated subtraction.

Equipment
coins

Notes

1. Ask the more able children to try to keep the number of steps to a minimum.

Q2 (a) 18 doughnuts, £1.98   (b) 25 shortcakes, £2.00   (c) 13 almond slices, £1.95

Q3 Change 9p. She spend £7.91 (791p). She bought 78 buns and cakes.

2. *Extend* by asking the children to plan for a party using local prices.

41

Worksheet 14 is a practice page of money problems.

Answers
1 (a) 30p (b) 48p (c) 28p (d) 60p (e) 65p
2 (a) 29p (b) 18p
3 (a) £2.60 (b) £2.71
4 3 weeks
5 (a) £1.20 (b) £1.80 (c) £2.40 (d) £3.00
   (e) 9 weeks

Page 72 Division practice

Number

Division practice
Use the method on page 66 to work these divisions.
Use as few steps as possible.

1	86 ÷ 7	2	105 ÷ 10	3	81 ÷ 3	4	97 ÷ 5
5	62 ÷ 4	6	110 ÷ 8	7	53 ÷ 2	8	121 ÷ 9
9	92 ÷ 3	10	89 ÷ 4	11	94 ÷ 10	12	75 ÷ 7
13	96 ÷ 8	14	156 ÷ 10	15	178 ÷ 9	16	154 ÷ 11

17 Clare and Dominic are making a balsa wood aeroplane. They cut strips of balsa wood 8 centimetres long. How many can they cut out from each of these lengths?
(a) 50 centimetres (b) 100 centimetres
(c) 75 centimetres (d) 112 centimetres
(e) 160 centimetres
How much is left each time?

18 Paul is helping to get ready for the school fête. He has a large box of 84 sweets which he is dividing into smaller packets of six sweets each. How many small packets can he make?
The large box of sweets costs 95p and Paul sells all the small packets for 10p each. How much money (profit) does he make for the school?

72

Content
Division problems and practice.

Notes
1. Encourage children to use the method of repeated subtractions. Some will use repeated addition.
2. Some children should be encouraged to use as few steps as is practical. Others will need to use more steps until they have gained confidence.

Q1 12 and 2 left   Q2 10 and 5 left
Q3 27   Q4 19 and 2 left
Q5 15 and 2 left   Q6 13 and 6 left
Q7 26 and 1 left   Q8 13 and 4 left
Q9 30 and 2 left   Q10 22 and 1 left
Q11 9 and 4 left   Q12 10 and 5 left
Q13 12   Q14 15 and 6 left
Q15 19 and 7 left   Q16 14
Q17 (a) 6 and 2 cm left
    (b) 12 and 4 cm left
    (c) 9 and 3 cm left
    (d) 14
    (e) 20
Q18 14 packets 45p

Worksheet 15 is a puzzle with clues that give practice and consolidation of division work.

Answers

21	23	27	16	28
y	o	u	d	e
18	28	19	22	28
s	e	r	v	e
15	17	19	18	24
f	i	r	s	t
25	19	17	32	28
p	r	i	z	e

Message: You deserve first prize.

42

Shape

Page 73 Round and round
Page 74 Matching shapes

Content
Investigating shapes with rotational symmetry.

Vocabulary
rotational symmetry, centre of rotation, angle of turn

Equipment
plastic or metal templates, stiff paper, unbreakable mirrors, red pens, scissors

Notes

1. If plastic or metal templates are not available, use stiff card.

2. Regular shapes (squares, etc) have both mirror and rotational symmetry. Here we are concentrating on rotational symmetry.

3. Make sure that the children do not cut into the paper surrounding the shapes when cutting them out.

4. One edge of each shape and one edge of the hole are coloured so that the children can count the different positions that are possible. Some children will notice that the number of positions is the same as the number of edges in each shape (although you may have to question them about this).

5. On page 74, one half of the sheet of paper (diagonal cut) is not the mirror image of the other half. This can be checked by folding along the diagonal. However, when one triangular half is turned about the centre of the sheet of paper through half a turn, it coincides with the other half. The two pieces do *not* coincide when the sheet of paper is folded along the diagonal. When a rectangle is divided in half along a diagonal, the two halves have rotational symmetry. Turning is the only way of making the two halves (triangles) coincide. Let the children try turning one triangle about any points they suggest.

6. Ask the children if the diagonal is a mirror line. Reinforce that the centre of the sheet of paper is the centre of rotation.

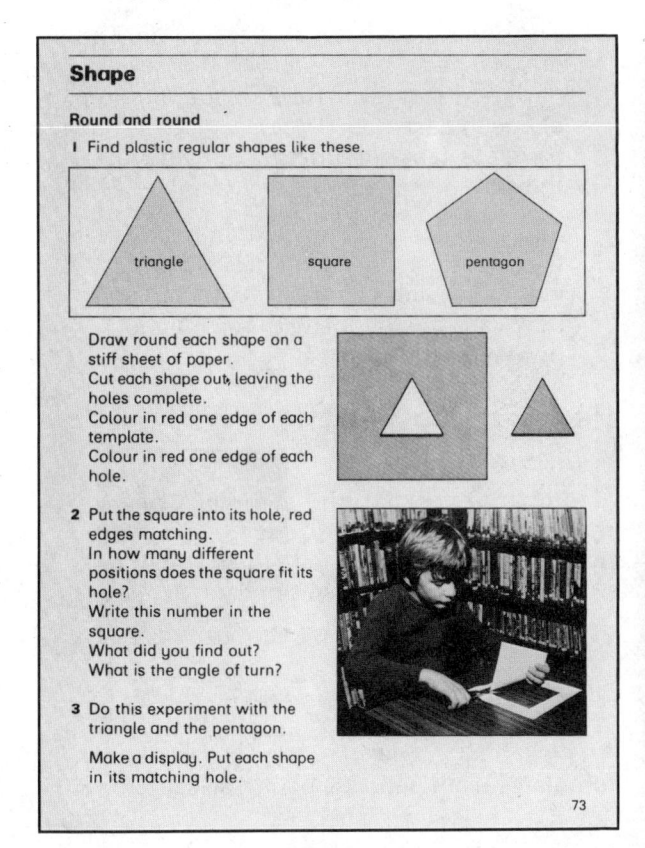

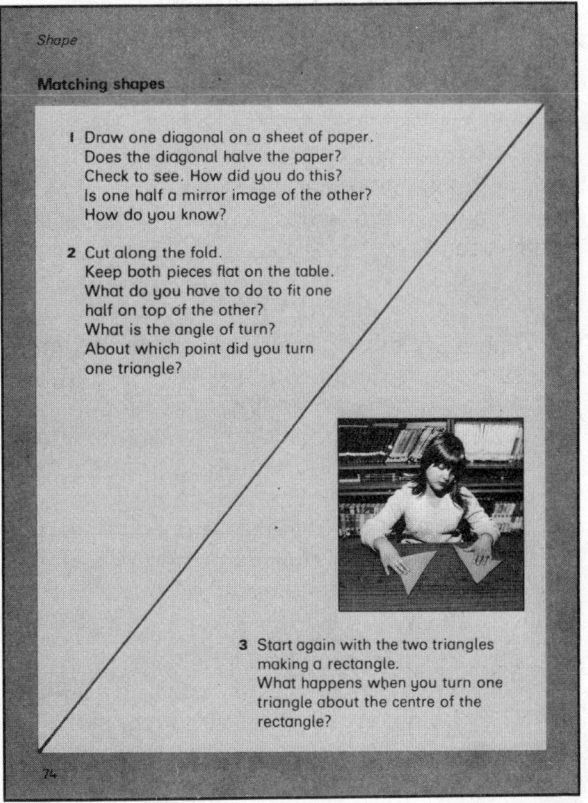

Shape

Round and round

1 Find plastic regular shapes like these.

triangle   square   pentagon

Draw round each shape on a stiff sheet of paper.
Cut each shape out, leaving the holes complete.
Colour in red one edge of each template.
Colour in red one edge of each hole.

2 Put the square into its hole, red edges matching.
In how many different positions does the square fit its hole?
Write this number in the square.
What did you find out?
What is the angle of turn?

3 Do this experiment with the triangle and the pentagon.

Make a display. Put each shape in its matching hole.

73

Shape

Matching shapes

1 Draw one diagonal on a sheet of paper.
Does the diagonal halve the paper?
Check to see. How did you do this?
Is one half a mirror image of the other?
How do you know?

2 Cut along the fold.
Keep both pieces flat on the table.
What do you have to do to fit one half on top of the other?
What is the angle of turn?
About which point did you turn one triangle?

3 Start again with the two triangles making a rectangle.
What happens when you turn one triangle about the centre of the rectangle?

74

Page 75 Match the edges

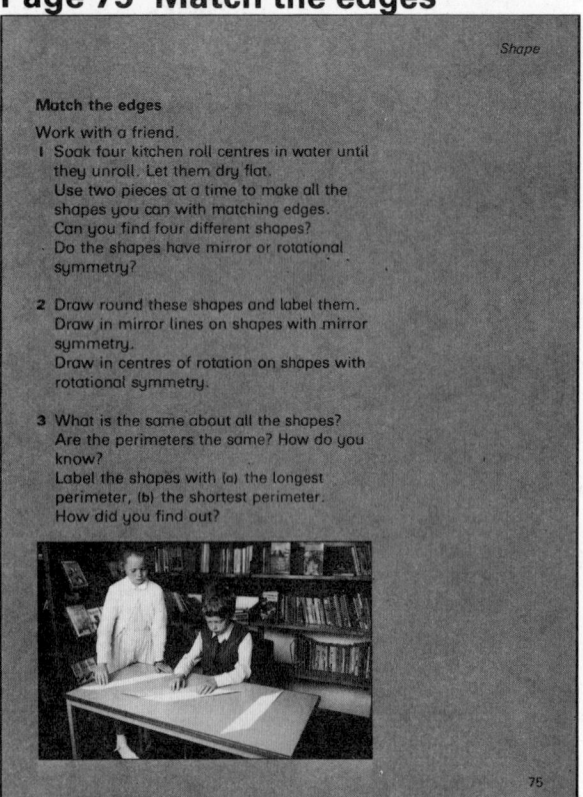

> **Match the edges**
>
> Work with a friend.
> 1. Soak four kitchen roll centres in water until they unroll. Let them dry flat.
>   Use two pieces at a time to make all the shapes you can with matching edges.
>   Can you find four different shapes?
>   Do the shapes have mirror or rotational symmetry?
>
> 2. Draw round these shapes and label them.
>   Draw in mirror lines on shapes with mirror symmetry.
>   Draw in centres of rotation on shapes with rotational symmetry.
>
> 3. What is the same about all the shapes?
>   Are the perimeters the same? How do you know?
>   Label the shapes with (a) the longest perimeter, (b) the shortest perimeter.
>   How did you find out?

Content
Using two identical shapes (parallelograms) to make shapes with rotational and mirror symmetry (conservation of area). Investigating perimeters.

Equipment
pairs of identical paper towel centres, bowl of water, paint and brushes (to paint identical faces if required)

Notes
1. There are four shapes: two with rotational symmetry (parallelograms) and two with mirror symmetry. To obtain the shapes with mirror symmetry one piece must be turned over. If the children do not think of turning one piece over, ask them what shapes they could make if they do this. Ask the children how they can check whether the shapes have rotational or mirror symmetry.

   Test for mirror symmetry
   Fold one piece along the matching edge. The two pieces coincide for mirror symmetry.

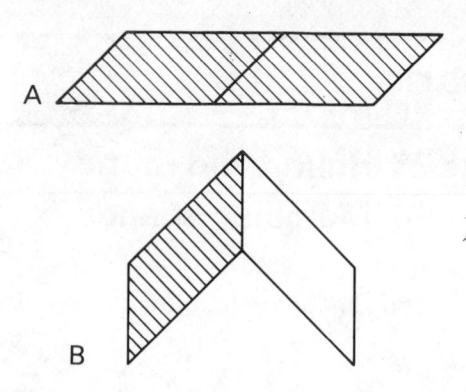

   Test for rotational symmetry
   Turn one piece flat on the table about the centre of the matching edge until the two pieces coincide (half a turn in example A).

   Q.3 The children may use string to compare perimeters. If so, ask if they can also find the longest perimeter without using string.

2. The children may not immediately realise that the areas of all the shapes are the same because each shape is made of two identical pieces. If they do not think of this, ask them, 'What is the same about all the pieces?' Try to prompt rather than giving the answer yourself.

3. The perimeters are not all the same. There are two pairs of shapes with the same perimeters, one mirror and one rotational shape in each pair. The two shapes shown have the same perimeters (they have 'lost' the shorter edges).

4. *Extend* by asking the children to use the two identical pieces to make shapes without matching edges. Ask, 'Can you make another shape with the longest perimeter/the shortest perimeter?'

Page 76 How many lines?

Content
Finding the axes of mirror symmetry of a regular triangle, a square, a rectangle and a pentagon. Comparison with the number of positions of rotational symmetry.

Vocabulary
axis, axes

Equipment
templates from page 73, paper, scissors

Shape

How many lines?

Use the templates from page 73 to cut out these shapes from paper.

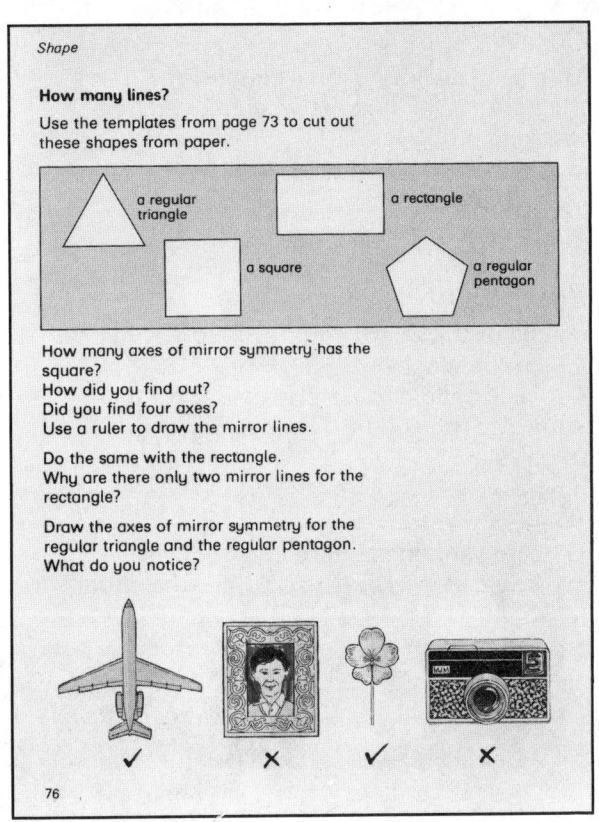

a regular triangle   a rectangle   a square   a regular pentagon

How many axes of mirror symmetry has the square?
How did you find out?
Did you find four axes?
Use a ruler to draw the mirror lines.

Do the same with the rectangle.
Why are there only two mirror lines for the rectangle?

Draw the axes of mirror symmetry for the regular triangle and the regular pentagon.
What do you notice?

✓   ✗   ✓   ✗

Notes

1. Precede by giving the children paper and scissors and asking them to cut a shape with one axis of mirror symmetry.

2. The paper shapes should be cut carefully, using the templates from page 73. Paper is used so that the axes of mirror symmetry can be found by folding – try to get the children to suggest folding to obtain these axes. Make sure that they find all the axes, eg ask, 'How can you check the shape for mirror symmetry?'

3. The regular triangle has three mirror lines and the square has four (two diagonals). The rectangle has only two mirror lines. Its two diagonals divide the rectangle into two parts which have rotational symmetry. The regular pentagon has five axes of mirror symmetry.

4. *Extend* to the hexagon. Then ask the children, 'How many rotations of the triangle bring it back to its starting position?' How many axes of mirror symmetry has it?'
Repeat this for the square, the pentagon and the hexagon. Ask the children what they notice. (In regular shapes, the edges are all equal, the angles are equal, and the number of axes of mirror symmetry is the same as the number of positions of rotational symmetry.) Collect containers of different shapes, if possible with lids, eg octagons, hexagons, rubbings of tiles (such as those on some doorsteps); and shapes which are not regular, such as isosceles triangles and parallelograms.

Worksheet 16 gives consolidation and extension work on mirror symmetry.

Answer

1 H, O, X

Page 77 Reducing shapes

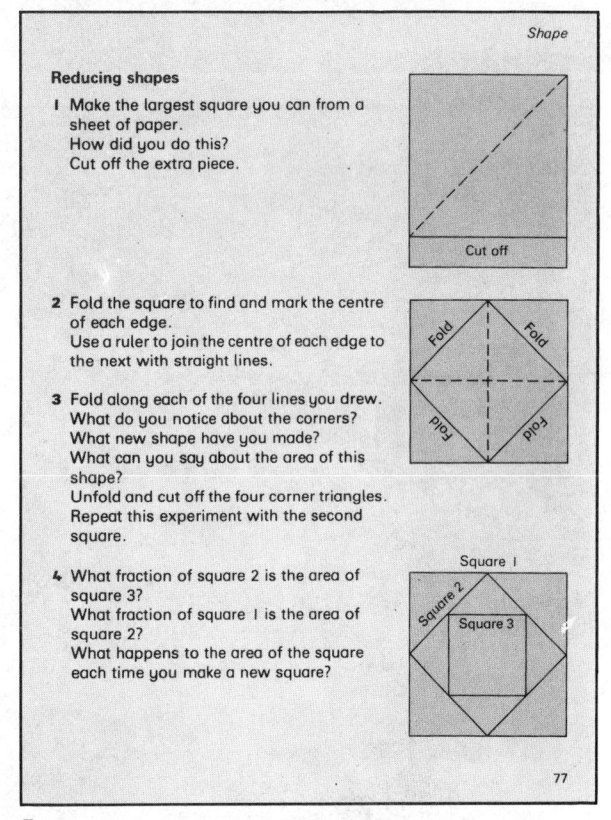

Shape

Reducing shapes

1 Make the largest square you can from a sheet of paper.
How did you do this?
Cut off the extra piece.

2 Fold the square to find and mark the centre of each edge.
Use a ruler to join the centre of each edge to the next with straight lines.

3 Fold along each of the four lines you drew.
What do you notice about the corners?
What new shape have you made?
What can you say about the area of this shape?
Unfold and cut off the four corner triangles. Repeat this experiment with the second square.

4 What fraction of square 2 is the area of square 3?
What fraction of square 1 is the area of square 2?
What happens to the area of the square each time you make a new square?

Content

Making a square. By repeated folding, making a series of smaller squares.

Vocabulary

reducing

Equipment

plain thin paper, scissors, rulers

Notes

1. Notice how the children make the largest

square. They should match adjacent edges – but try not to tell them.

2. The corners should all meet at the centre. Therefore the new square and the corner triangles have the same area. The area of square 2 is half that of square 1.

3. Ask the children to write about their findings; eg each time the area of the new square is half that of the previous square. The sequence is $\frac{1}{2}, \frac{1}{4}, \frac{1}{8}$.
Ask the children to describe, verbally or in writing, what is happening.
Ask, 'Are all the squares the same shape? How do you know?'

Pages 78 and 79 Bigger and bigger

Content
Enlarging 2-dimensional shapes and finding the patterns of successive areas and perimeters.

Vocabulary
dimension

Equipment
plastic or thick card squares (edge 2 cm or 2.5 cm or 1 inch)
Let each child choose one colour for his squares. The children can work individually or in pairs.

Notes
Q1 The sequence of areas of successive squares is 1, 4, 9, 16, 25, 36 – the square

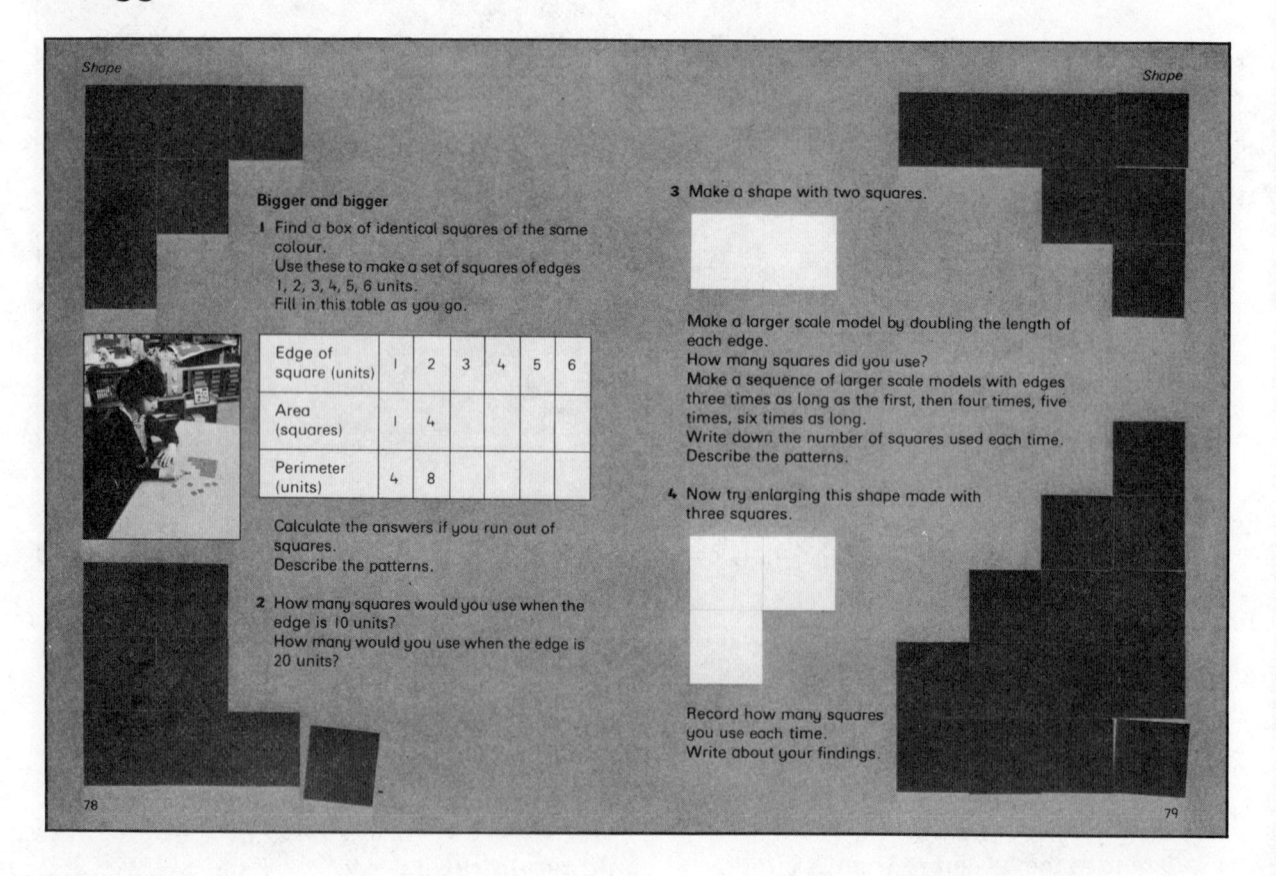

Bigger and bigger

1 Find a box of identical squares of the same colour.
Use these to make a set of squares of edges 1, 2, 3, 4, 5, 6 units.
Fill in this table as you go.

Edge of square (units)	1	2	3	4	5	6
Area (squares)	1	4				
Perimeter (units)	4	8				

Calculate the answers if you run out of squares.
Describe the patterns.

2 How many squares would you use when the edge is 10 units?
How many would you use when the edge is 20 units?

3 Make a shape with two squares.

Make a larger scale model by doubling the length of each edge.
How many squares did you use?
Make a sequence of larger scale models with edges three times as long as the first, then four times, five times, six times as long.
Write down the number of squares used each time.
Describe the patterns.

4 Now try enlarging this shape made with three squares.

Record how many squares you use each time.
Write about your findings.

46

numbers. The sequence of perimeters is 4, 8, 12, 16, 20, 24. Ask the children to describe each sequence. The squares increase by odd numbers. The perimeters increase by 4. The perimeters are multiples of 4.

Q3 Either pattern can be used at first. Use each pattern in turn.

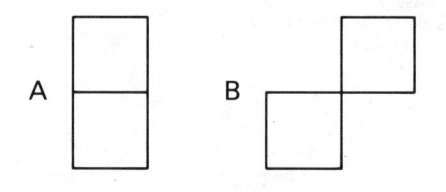

A B

The areas are 2, 8, 18, 32, 50, 72 squares. (If each area is divided by 2, successive ratios are 1, 4, 9, 16, 25, 36, the same ratios as for the squares.)
The perimeters for A are 6, 12, 18, 24, 30, 36 units.

Q4 Areas are 3, 12, 27, 48, 75, 108 squares. Perimeters are 8, 16, 24, 32, 40, 48 units.

Length

Page 80 Finding the perimeter

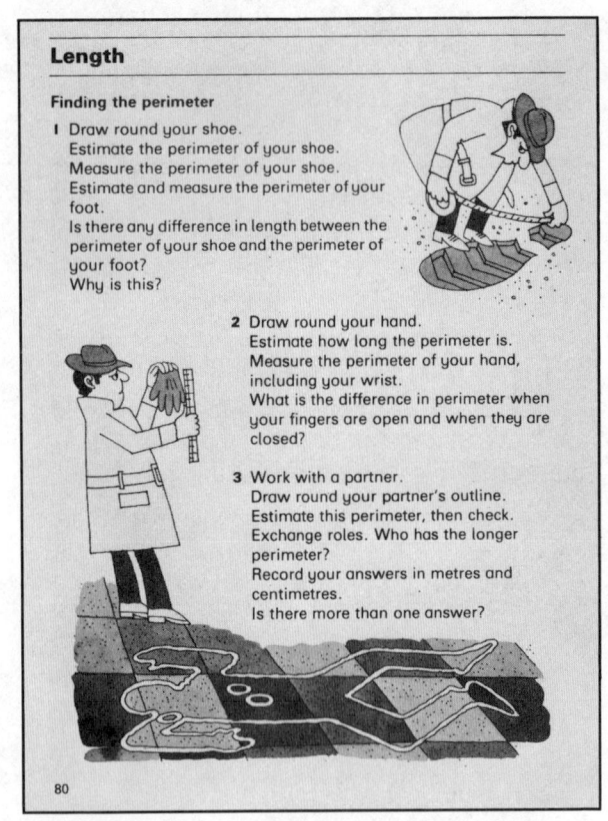

> **Length**
>
> **Finding the perimeter**
>
> 1. Draw round your shoe.
>   Estimate the perimeter of your shoe.
>   Measure the perimeter of your shoe.
>   Estimate and measure the perimeter of your foot.
>   Is there any difference in length between the perimeter of your shoe and the perimeter of your foot?
>   Why is this?
>
> 2. Draw round your hand.
>   Estimate how long the perimeter is.
>   Measure the perimeter of your hand, including your wrist.
>   What is the difference in perimeter when your fingers are open and when they are closed?
>
> 3. Work with a partner.
>   Draw round your partner's outline.
>   Estimate this perimeter, then check.
>   Exchange roles. Who has the longer perimeter?
>   Record your answers in metres and centimetres.
>   Is there more than one answer?

Content
Measuring and comparing perimeters.

Vocabulary
exchange roles

Equipment
2-metre measures, large sheets of paper

Notes
1. Measures should be in centimetres, or in metres/centimetres to the nearest whole centimetre.

2. When measuring the perimeter of their outlines, the children will need to use two measures end to end.

Q3 The children should lie with heels together and hands by their sides. There will still be more than one perimeter; eg measuring from front to back (via the nose!) rather than round the sides.

Page 81 Ratio

> *Length*
>
> **Ratio**
>
> Use squared paper to draw these rectangles and squares.
>
> length twice the width
> $$\text{ratio} = \frac{\text{length}}{\text{width}} = \frac{2}{1}$$
>
> length 3 times the width
> $$\text{ratio} = \frac{\text{length}}{\text{width}} = \frac{3}{1}$$
>
> length $1\frac{1}{2}$ times the width
> $$\text{ratio} = \frac{\text{length}}{\text{width}} = \frac{3}{2}$$
>
> 1. Can you find a room in your school which is square?
>   What is the ratio of the length and width of a square?
>
> 2. Can you find a picture which is twice as long as it is wide?
>   What is the ratio of its edges?
>
> 3. Can you find a room which is half as wide as it is long?
>   What is the ratio of the edges of such a room?
>
> 4. Use squared paper to cut rectangles with these ratios of edges.
>   (a) $\frac{2}{1}$ (b) $\frac{3}{1}$ (c) $\frac{3}{2}$ (d) $\frac{1}{1}$ (e) $\frac{1}{4}$ (f) $\frac{4}{3}$
>   Label each rectangle with the ratio of its edges.

Content
Introducing the ratio of two lengths.

Vocabulary
ratio (comparison by division)

Equipment
centimetre squared paper, scissors, paper with larger squares (eg 2 cm)

Notes
1. Before the children use standard measures to find whether a room is square or not, ask if they could use another method to discover this (eg using a ball of string; counting squares on the floor or ceiling, or bricks on the walls; or pacing).

2. Before the children measure the edges of the room, discuss the unit of measure and appropriate approximation, eg measure to

the nearest decimetre, giving answers in metres/decimetres, because centimetres are too small.

Note You will probably find that the children measure across or down the centre of the room rather than along the edges. If they do this, ask them to find whether a box, such as a biscuit tin, is square or not, and watch what they do.

3. *Extend* by providing paper with larger squares from which to cut rectangles. Ask if these rectangles are the same shape as those cut from centimetre squared paper.

Worksheet 17 provides further practice on ratios.

Answers

1 $\frac{4}{2}$ 2 $\frac{5}{3}$ 3 $\frac{1}{4}$ 4 $\frac{2}{2}$ 5 $\frac{8}{4}$ 6 $\frac{3}{4}$

Page 82 Round and round again

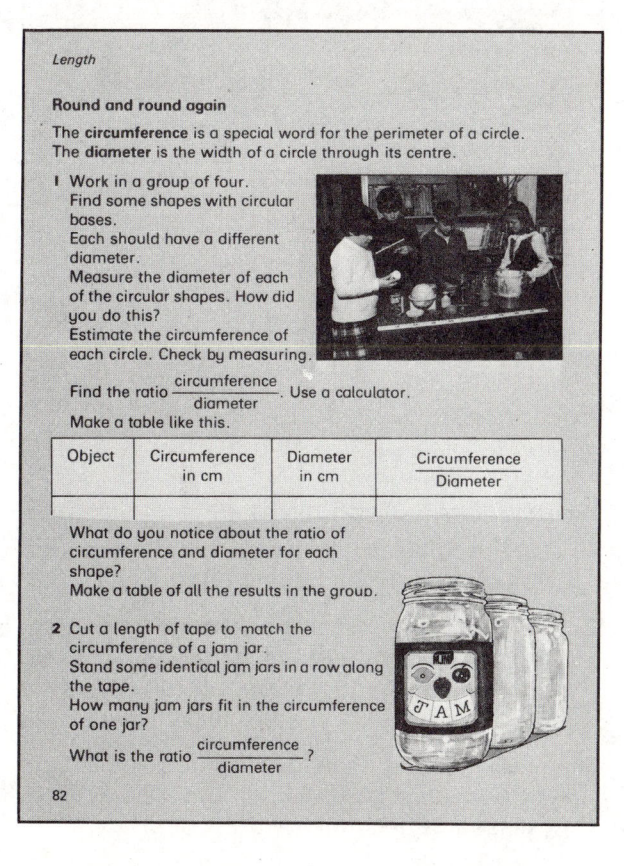

Content
Introducing the ratio of the perimeter (circumference) and diameter of circles.

Vocabulary
circumference, diameter, ratio, circular

Equipment
metre strips, objects with circular base, tape, scissors, jam jars

Notes
1. Try to make a collection of circular objects with diameters which are a whole number of centimetres (to make them easier to measure).

2. At first, children usually estimate the circumference to be twice the diameter.

Q2 It is sufficient for children to find that the circumference is '3 and a bit times the diameter'.

3. *Extend* by providing objects with diameters that are not a whole number of centimetres, but only if an electronic calculator is available. Otherwise the calculations are too difficult.

Page 83 Measuring in decimetres and centimetres

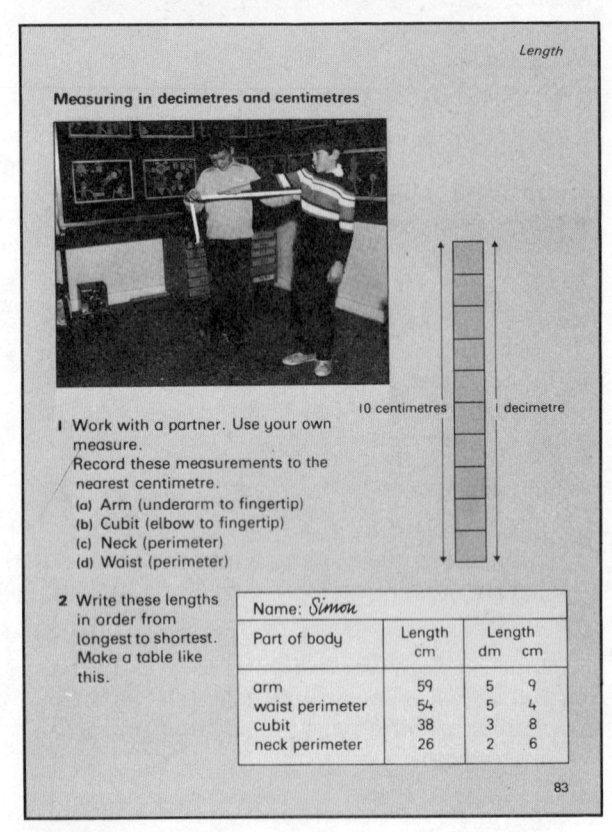

Length

Measuring in decimetres and centimetres

1. Work with a partner. Use your own measure. Record these measurements to the nearest centimetre.
   (a) Arm (underarm to fingertip)
   (b) Cubit (elbow to fingertip)
   (c) Neck (perimeter)
   (d) Waist (perimeter)

10 centimetres | 1 decimetre

2. Write these lengths in order from longest to shortest. Make a table like this.

Name: Simon

Part of body	Length cm	Length dm	cm
arm	59	5	9
waist perimeter	54	5	4
cubit	38	3	8
neck perimeter	26	2	6

Content
Measuring in decimetres and centimetres and arranging lengths in order.

Equipment
metre strips, 2-metre measures

Notes
1. Metre/centimetre strips, with decimetres clearly marked, can be used.
2. Precede by questioning children about the relations between centimetres, decimetres and metres.
3. Measurements should be to the nearest centimetre.

Page 84 Find the difference

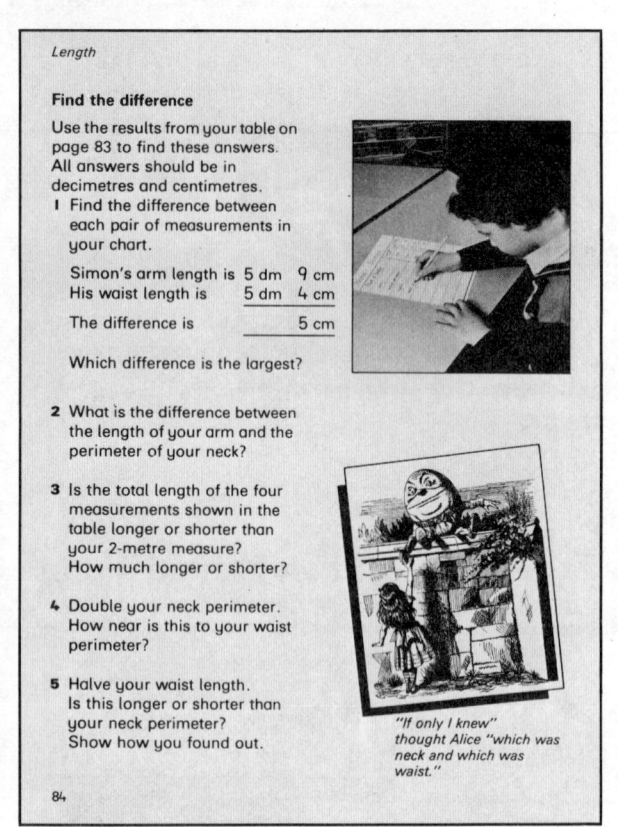

Length

Find the difference

Use the results from your table on page 83 to find these answers. All answers should be in decimetres and centimetres.

1. Find the difference between each pair of measurements in your chart.

   Simon's arm length is 5 dm 9 cm
   His waist length is   5 dm 4 cm
   The difference is   5 cm

   Which difference is the largest?

2. What is the difference between the length of your arm and the perimeter of your neck?

3. Is the total length of the four measurements shown in the table longer or shorter than your 2-metre measure? How much longer or shorter?

4. Double your neck perimeter. How near is this to your waist perimeter?

5. Halve your waist length. Is this longer or shorter than your neck perimeter? Show how you found out.

"If only I knew" thought Alice "which was neck and which was waist."

Content
Using the lengths measured on the preceding page for comparison, applying the four operations.

Equipment
2-metre measures

Notes
1. Let the children use their 2-metre measures if necessary when finding differences.
2. The waist perimeter is approximately twice the neck perimeter (application of ratio). Use the word 'ratio' in discussion and encourage the children to use this word.
3. This activity is used in Number (page 90) to introduce decimals (eg centimetres expressed as decimal fractions of a decimetre).

Pages 85 and 86 Checkpoint

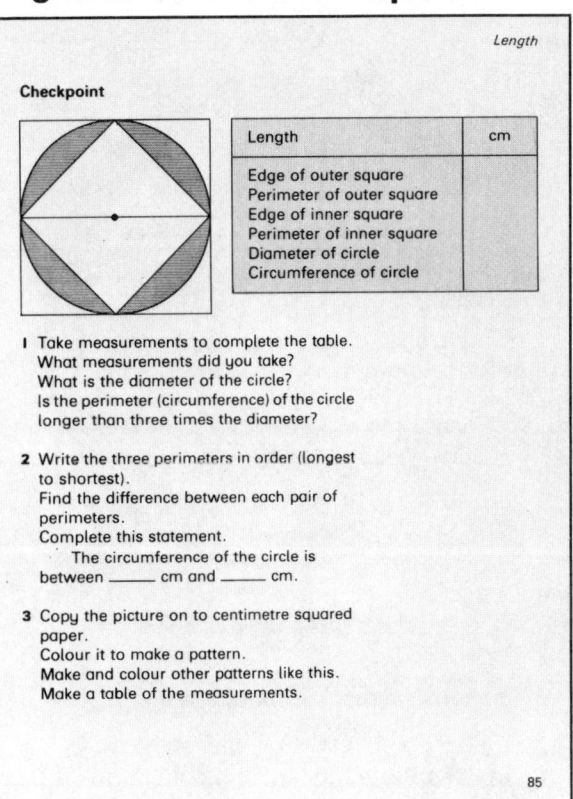

Checkpoint

Length	cm
Edge of outer square	
Perimeter of outer square	
Edge of inner square	
Perimeter of inner square	
Diameter of circle	
Circumference of circle	

1 Take measurements to complete the table.
What measurements did you take?
What is the diameter of the circle?
Is the perimeter (circumference) of the circle longer than three times the diameter?

2 Write the three perimeters in order (longest to shortest).
Find the difference between each pair of perimeters.
Complete this statement.
  The circumference of the circle is between ____ cm and ____ cm.

3 Copy the picture on to centimetre squared paper.
Colour it to make a pattern.
Make and colour other patterns like this.
Make a table of the measurements.

85

---

4 The edge of this table mat is to be bound with coloured tape.
Work in a group of four.
Each estimate the length of tape needed.
Each cut a paper strip of your estimated length.
Use your strip to check how near you were.
Was your estimate longer or shorter than the actual circumference?

5 Join your four perimeter strips without overlap.
If all four estimates were equal, what would the estimate be?
How did you find out?
Write about what you did.

6 Cut a strip to match the actual circumference of the mat.
Measure the strip and record the length.
Measure a diameter of the mat, and record it.
Find and record a length three times as long as the diameter.
Write down the difference between this length and the circumference of the mat.

86

Content
Checking that the children (a) can make measurements to the nearest centimetre; (b) can arrange the measurements in order of length and find the difference between them; (c) can find average lengths by folding.

Vocabulary
circumference, diameter

Equipment
metre strips marked in centimetres (or tape measures), centimetre squared paper, paints or coloured pencils, coloured paper strips 1 cm wide and 60 cm long, scissors, masking tape

Notes
Q1 Notice whether the children find perimeters of the squares by measuring one edge and multiplying by 4, or by measuring the whole perimeter. They can use string or paper strips to find the circumference of the circle.

Q2 The perimeters are:
   outer square = 24 cm
   circle = 19 cm
   inner square = 17 cm
Difference between outer square and circle = 5 cm
Difference between circle and inner square = 2 cm

1. Precede questions 4 to 6 by discussing with the children the degree of accuracy which is reasonable for the measurements (to the nearest centimetre).

Q4 Check that each child writes his name on the strip he estimates.

Q5 Check that the four strips (estimated) are joined end to end with masking tape. If the children hesitate, ask them what fraction each estimate would be if the four estimates were equal. If they say 'one quarter', ask, 'How can you find one quarter of this long strip?'

Q6 Suggest that the children make a table of their measurements. The circumference should be just over 2 cm longer than three times the diameter.

2. *Extend* by repeating question 6 with circles of different diameters, eg 10 cm, 12 cm, etc.

51

Number

Page 87 Fun with numbers

Content
Three number puzzles, involving addition and subtraction.

Vocabulary
solution

Equipment
cards numbered 1 to 6

Notes
1. The children will find it helpful if the numbers are on cards so that they can be moved around.

Q1 There are three basically different solutions.

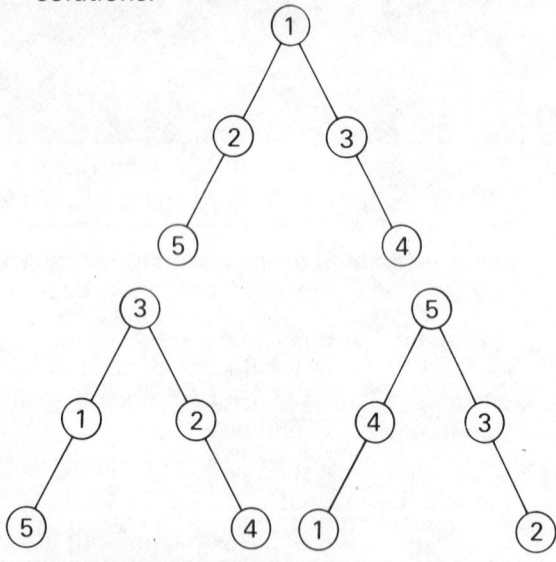

Q2 Here are two possible solutions. The sum of the numbers used is 15.

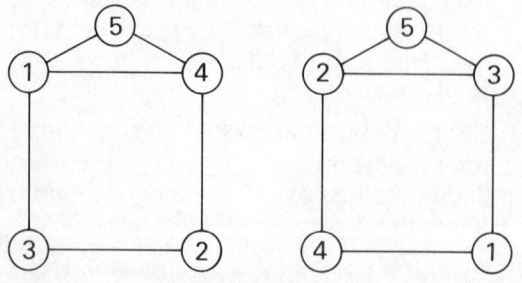

There are other solutions.

Q3 One solution is shown in the figure.

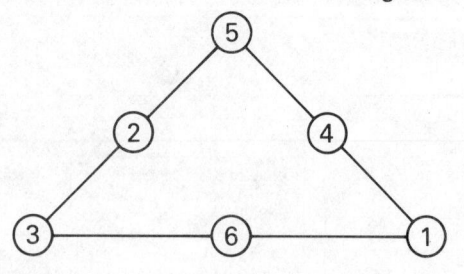

To find a different solution change the numbers to odd in the middle circles. The solution then is as follows.

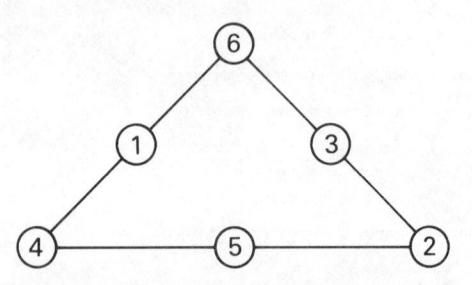

The sum of the numbers used is 21.

2. *Extend* by asking the children to make similar puzzles for a class collection.

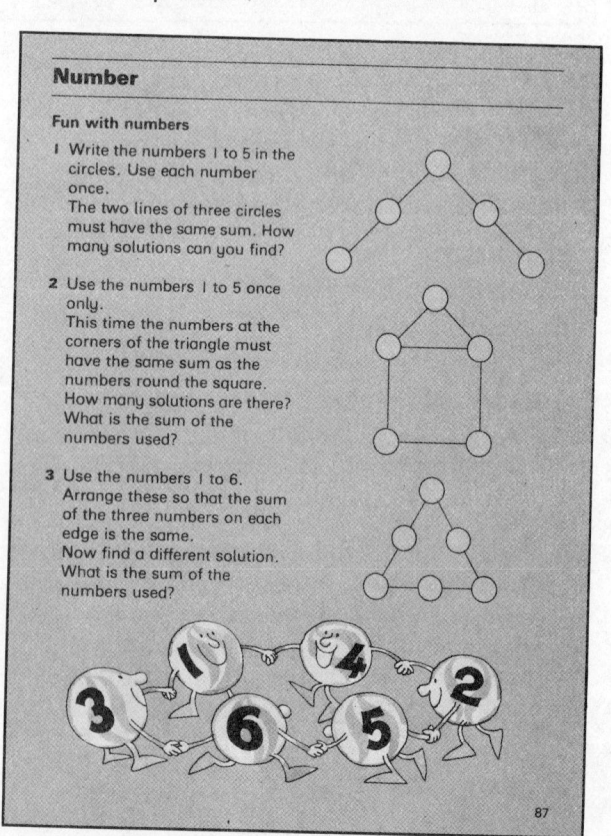

Number

Fun with numbers

1 Write the numbers 1 to 5 in the circles. Use each number once.
The two lines of three circles must have the same sum. How many solutions can you find?

2 Use the numbers 1 to 5 once only.
This time the numbers at the corners of the triangle must have the same sum as the numbers round the square. How many solutions are there? What is the sum of the numbers used?

3 Use the numbers 1 to 6. Arrange these so that the sum of the three numbers on each edge is the same.
Now find a different solution. What is the sum of the numbers used?

Pages 88 and 89 Perimeter patterns

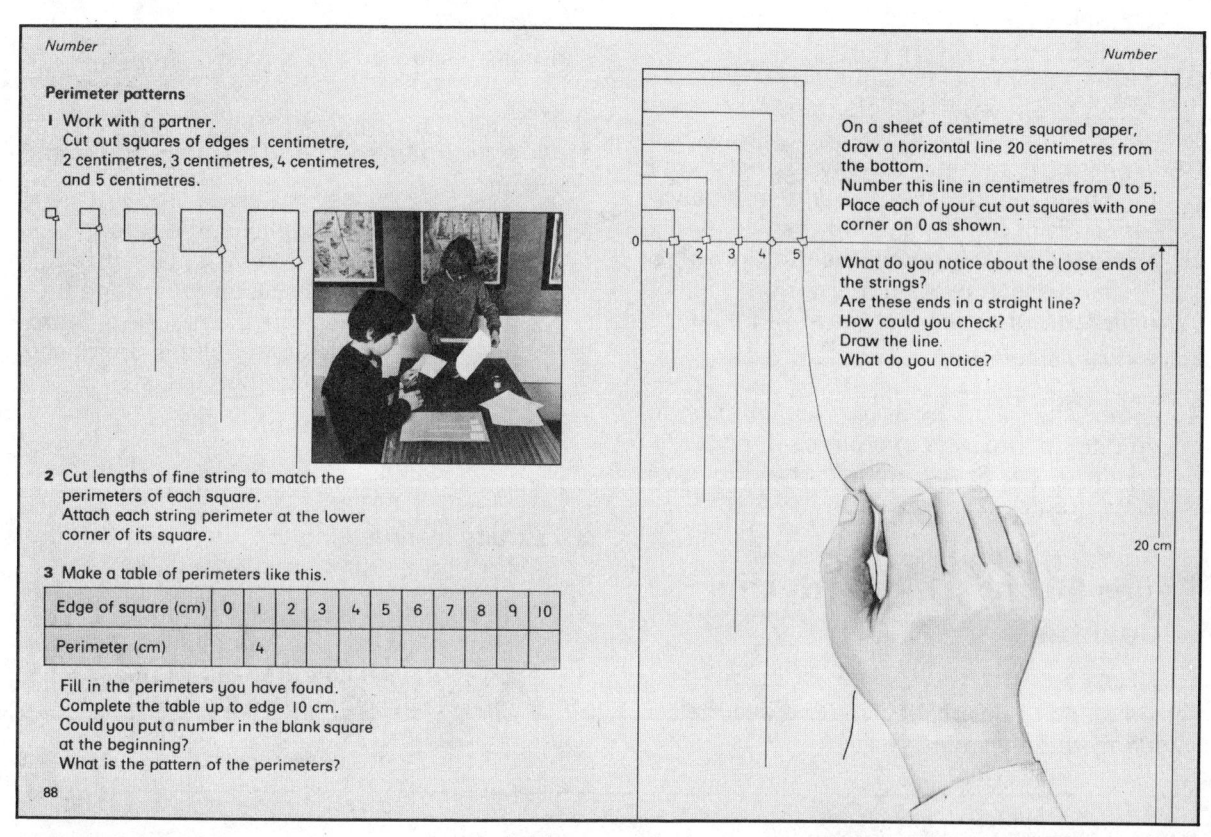

Page 88

Number

Perimeter patterns

1. Work with a partner.
   Cut out squares of edges 1 centimetre, 2 centimetres, 3 centimetres, 4 centimetres, and 5 centimetres.

2. Cut lengths of fine string to match the perimeters of each square.
   Attach each string perimeter at the lower corner of its square.

3. Make a table of perimeters like this.

Edge of square (cm)	0	1	2	3	4	5	6	7	8	9	10
Perimeter (cm)		4									

Fill in the perimeters you have found.
Complete the table up to edge 10 cm.
Could you put a number in the blank square at the beginning?
What is the pattern of the perimeters?

Number

On a sheet of centimetre squared paper, draw a horizontal line 20 centimetres from the bottom.
Number this line in centimetres from 0 to 5.
Place each of your cut out squares with one corner on 0 as shown.

What do you notice about the loose ends of the strings?
Are these ends in a straight line?
How could you check?
Draw the line.
What do you notice?

20 cm

Content
Finding the relationship between the edge of a square and its perimeter.
Showing graphically the relationship between the edge length of a square and its perimeter.

Vocabulary
vertical

Equipment
centimetre squared paper, string, strong adhesive or sellotape

Notes

1. Some children will find attaching the string to one corner of the square difficult. Let them, working in groups, make a display of the sequence of squares and their perimeters.

2. Some children will recognise that the perimeters are successive multiples of 4. Others will be able to see that the perimeter is the length of one edge multiplied by 4. A few children will write 0 in the blank square. Many will not think of zero.

Edge of square (cm)	Perimeter (cm)
0	0
1	4
2	8
3	12
4	16
5	20
6	24
7	28
8	32
9	36
10	40

3. *Extend* (a) by asking the children to find the length of the edge when the perimeter is known; (b) by asking some children to continue the sequence of perimeters.

Q4 It is important that the squares are superimposed as shown in the diagram.

Q5 When the diagram is displayed on the wall, the string lengths should hang vertically. The ends of the string should all lie in a straight line. Ask the children to draw this line and describe the pattern. Some children will notice that the straight line goes through 0.

4. *Extend* this work by asking the children to find the perimeters of squares of edges $1\frac{1}{2}$ cm, $2\frac{1}{2}$ cm, $3\frac{1}{2}$ cm, etc and entering these on a graph.

Pages 90 and 91 Introducing decimals

Content
Introduction to decimals using the decimetre. Working with decimals.

Vocabulary
decimal

Equipment
centimetre squared paper, crayons or paints

Notes
1. Ask the children to find the sum of ·1 and ·9, etc.

2. At this stage, for simplicity, the zero in front of the decimal point is not used, ie 0·1 is shown as ·1. (The reason for writing 0·1 is to show that there are 0 units. Also, there is a risk that the decimal point is unnoticed unless numbers are written 0·3, etc.)

Q6 Results should be recorded like this:
   1 − ·3 = ·7
   1 − ·7 = ·3

3. *Extend* by repeating the work with ·6dm, ·7dm, ·8dm, ·9dm.

4. A display should be made of all the decimetre strips, uncut but with a different section of each coloured, as on pages 90 and 91. These should be labelled
   ·1 + ·9 = 1,   ·2 + ·8 = 1, etc.

Number

Introducing decimals

1. Use centimetre squared paper.
Cut five strips of paper, each 1 centimetre wide and 1 decimetre long.
Colour 1 centimetre of one strip like this.

$\frac{1}{10}$ dm $\frac{9}{10}$ dm

2. How many centimetres are there in a decimetre?
What fraction of 1 decimetre is 1 centimetre?
What fraction is coloured? What fraction is not coloured?

3. A short way of writing $\frac{1}{10}$ is ·1 (point 1).
· is called a decimal point. It divides units from tenths of units.
What is the short way of writing $\frac{9}{10}$?

·1   ·9

4. Cut off the coloured part (·1 dm). What length is left?
Record like this: ·1 + ·9 = 1 and ·9 + ·1 = 1
                   1 − ·1 = ·9 and 1 − ·9 = ·1

5. From a second strip, cut off 2 centimetres.
What decimal of 1 decimetre is this?
What decimal is left?

·2   ·8

Record like this:
1 − ·2 = ·8
1 − ·8 = ·2

6. Use another strip. This time, cut off 3 centimetres.
What decimal of 1 decimetre is this?
What decimal is left?
Record as above.

·3   ·7

7. Continue, cutting off first ·4, then ·5.

8. Trace the large rectangle and on it mark what decimal of a decimetre each part is. The first one has been done for you.

1 dm
1 whole
·1   ·9

1 whole

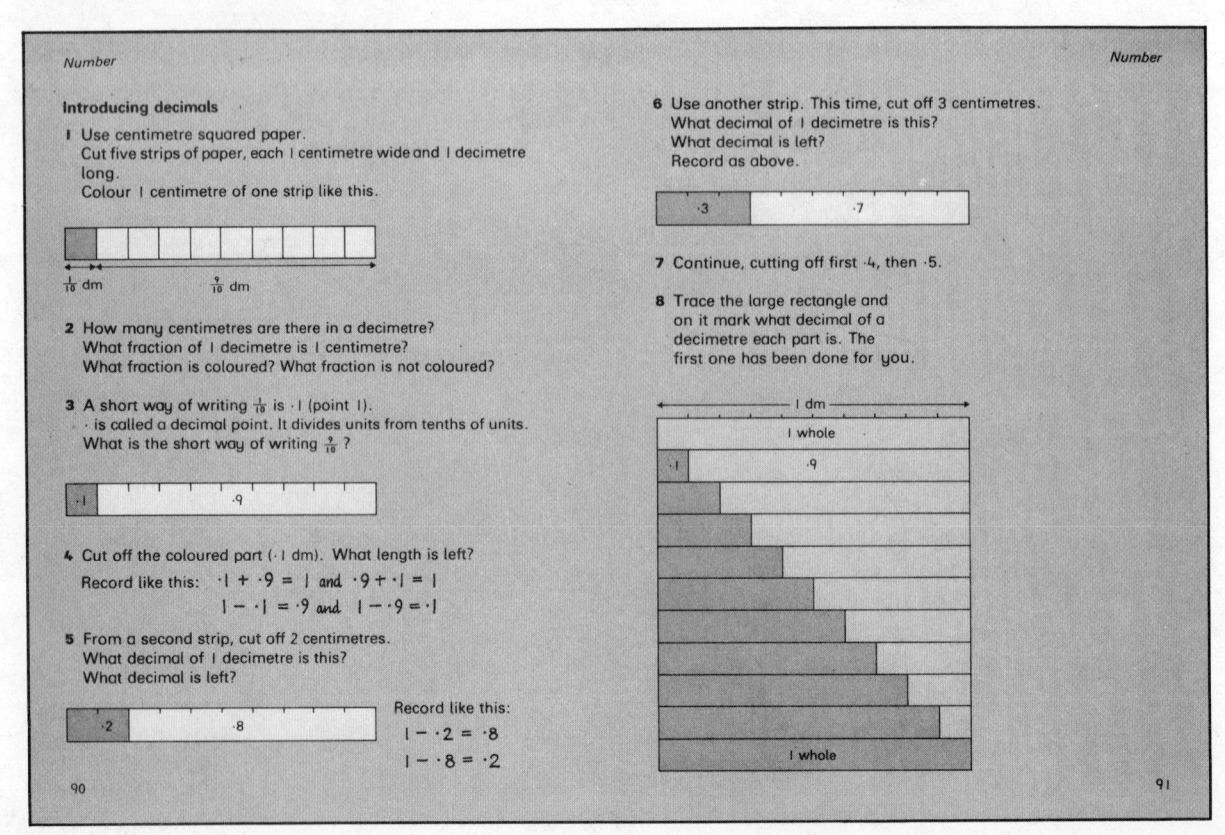

90   91

Time

Page 92 Morning and afternoon

Content
Referring to am and pm, midday (noon) and midnight.

Vocabulary
am (ante meridian), pm (post meridian), midday, noon, midnight

Equipment
clock templates

Notes
1. Suggest that the children make an illustrated diary. Clocks should be drawn to show all the times mentioned in the diary. Ask the children to write these times in two different ways, eg 8 am or 8 o'clock in the morning.

2. Ask the children to say how much time has elapsed between the time on one clock face and that on the next.

Worksheet 18 can be used at this stage for general revision if necessary.

Page 93 Measuring shadows

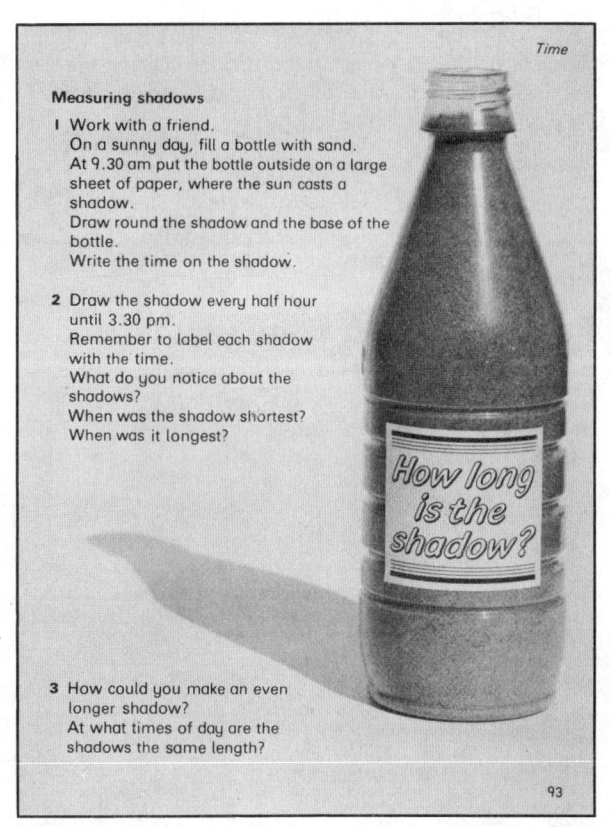

Content
Drawing shadows and associating these with times of day.

Equipment
plastic bottles ($\frac{3}{4}$ to 1 litre), dry sand (for weighting bottles)

Notes
1. Precede by taking the children outside and letting them observe their own shadows and those of a tree or building. Ask them how shadows are made.

2. Some children may find that the paper and bottle are lost in the shadow of the school building. If this happens, ask them to find a place which will not be overshadowed by buildings, etc.

3. The shadow will be at its shortest at 12 noon, or in British Summer Time at 1 pm. Shadows should be the same length at, for example, 9.30 am and 2.30 pm when shadows are shortest at 12 noon.

4. Ask the children if they can explain why their shadows are not the same shape and length all day long.

5. *Extend* by asking the children to draw round each other's shadows and shadows of trees, posts etc at half-hour intervals.

6. *Extend* by asking the children to find examples of 'clocks' which tell the time using shadows. Suggest they make a sundial themselves.

Page 94 When were you born?

Content
Introducing the seasons through birthday months.

Vocabulary
seasons

Equipment
class chart, matchboxes, sticky paper, paints, glue, scissors

Notes
1. This topic could form a class project which might take half a term or more.

2. Make a class chart with birthday months. Columns should allow enough room for one column of matchboxes.

3. Introduce the names and concept of seasons. Mark these on the birthday chart. Question the children frequently until they know the seasons. (The dates of the seasons have been simplified on the chart.)

4. Ask if there are any months with the same number of birthdays, and any seasons with the same number of birthdays. Link the work on seasons with weather observations of temperature outside and inside, wind direction, rain, snow, and clouds. Ask the children what else they can find from the chart. They could record their findings in a class birthday book.

5. Ask each child to collect the birthdays of his family and extended family. The children can then make their own family birthday charts. Ask them to try to collect at least one birthday for each season. Then ask them to make a chart with birthdays allocated to seasons instead of months.

6. *Extend* by asking the children to collect birthday months from other classes. The birthday chart can then be extended to include these.

Worksheet 19 provides consolidation and extension work on making and using a bar graph.

Answers
1 (a) 27 (b) 26
2 Monday and Thursday
3 Tuesday
4 5
5 135

Page 95 How long does it take?

Content
Finding the duration of television programmes.

Equipment
clocks with moveable hands, *Radio Times* and *TV Times* or newspapers with television programmes

Notes

1. Precede by giving the children practice in finding duration of time using their own clocks, eg ask them to show 10 o'clock, then 10.20. Ask, 'How many minutes have passed?' Make 10.35. Ask, 'How many minutes have passed since 10.20?' Make 11 o'clock. Ask, 'How much time has passed since 10.35?' Make 11.10. Ask, 'How much time has passed since 10.35?'

2. The children are not ready for work on this page until they can find duration of time within an hour.

How long does it take?

1 How long do these television programmes last? Make the times on your own clock if it helps.

Blue Peter starts at 5.05 pm and ends at 5.35 pm.
Play School starts at 3.55 pm and ends at 4.20 pm.
Scooby Doo starts at 4.40 pm and ends at 5.00 pm.
The Adventures of Morph starts at 5.35 pm and ends at 5.40 pm.

2 Arrange the programmes in order from the shortest to the longest.
Which programme starts at the earliest time?
Which one starts at the latest time?
How many programmes last less than half an hour?
How many last less than 15 minutes?

3 Which television programmes do you like best? Make a list. Include starting and finishing times and the lengths of the programmes. Make your own television guide from this.

Volume and capacity

Pages 96 and 97 Making cuboids

Content
Making (a) irregular shapes and (b) cuboids of the same volume, with interlocking cubes. Finding the 'skin' area of the shapes.

Vocabulary
dimensions

Results

Equipment
interlocking cubes

Notes
we could only make 3.

1. ESA interlocking cubes or Osmiroid centicubes can be used. Each pair of children needs up to 100 cubes. The staircase is a triangular number. The snake, whether made as a long cuboid or a zig-zag shape, will have more squares showing than other shapes. The shapes have the same volume but different surface ('skin') areas. These can be expressed as the number of squares showing, since not all interlocking cubes are in standard units.

Q1 The cuboids are 1 by 1 by 8   *H W L*
                  1 by 2 by 4 } units
                  2 by 2 by 2

'Skin areas' are 34 squares
              28 squares
              24 squares

Q3 The table, with dimensions in order of length, is:

Cuboid – volume 24 cubes		
Width units	Height units	Length units
1	1	24
1	2	12
1	3	8
1	4	6
2	2	6
2	3	4

Height doubled, length halved.
Height trebled, length one-third.
Height quadrupled, length quartered.
This is an inverse relation.

Volume and capacity

Making cuboids

Work with a friend. You need some interlocking cubes.

1. Make all the cuboids you can with 8 cubes. How are your cuboids alike? How are they different?
Work out the total number of *squares* showing for each cuboid. Which cuboid has (a) the smallest, (b) the largest, number of squares showing?

2. Take 10 cubes and make an irregular shape. Repeat this with two more sets of 10 cubes. Make each shape different.
Can you make a staircase with 10 cubes?
Can you make a snake?
What is the same about all your models? How are they different?
Which shape has most squares showing?

3. Build as many different cuboids as you can using 24 interlocking cubes each time. Make a table showing the cuboids.

Cuboids – volume 24 cubes		
Width units	Height units	Length units
1	1	24
1	2	—

The dimensions are in order of length.

When the height is doubled, what is the length?
When the height is trebled, what is the length?
Complete these statements.
   When the height is doubled, the length is ___.
   When the height is trebled, the length is ___.

4. Now, using not more than 36 cubes, try to make hollow shapes. Draw each shape and find the volume of the space inside.

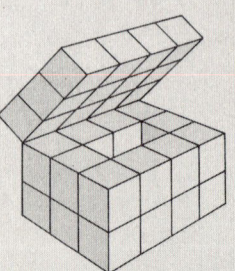

Height and length can be compared *only* when the width remains the same. Discuss this with the children.

Q4 Hollow shapes:
a 3 by 3 by 3 cube with space of one cube inside
a 3 by 3 by 4 cuboid with space of two cubes inside

Worksheet 20 gives further work on finding volumes of cuboids and other shapes using centimetre cubes.

Answers
1 3 cubes   4 cubes   4 cubes   3 cubes
2 (a) 8 cubes, 1 layer.   Volume 8 cubes
   (b) 4 cubes, 2 layers. Volume 8 cubes
   (c) 6 cubes, 2 layers. Volume 12 cubes
   (d) 4 cubes, 5 layers. Volume 20 cubes
   (e) 8 cubes, 3 layers. Volume 24 cubes
   (f) 9 cubes, 2 layers. Volume 18 cubes

Pages 98 and 99 Going to the doctor

Content
Working with millilitres.

Vocabulary
graduated, graduation

Equipment
medicine bottles (100 ml, 125 ml, 150 ml, 200 ml, 300 ml, 500 ml), medicine spoons, $\frac{1}{2}$-litre measure

Notes
1. If the medicine bottles are not made of plastic, provide a rubber or plastic mat for the sink.
2. It is a good idea for the teacher to supervise the group and listen to the children's answers.
3. Encourage the children to talk/write about their own experiences. Ask them to include quantities.

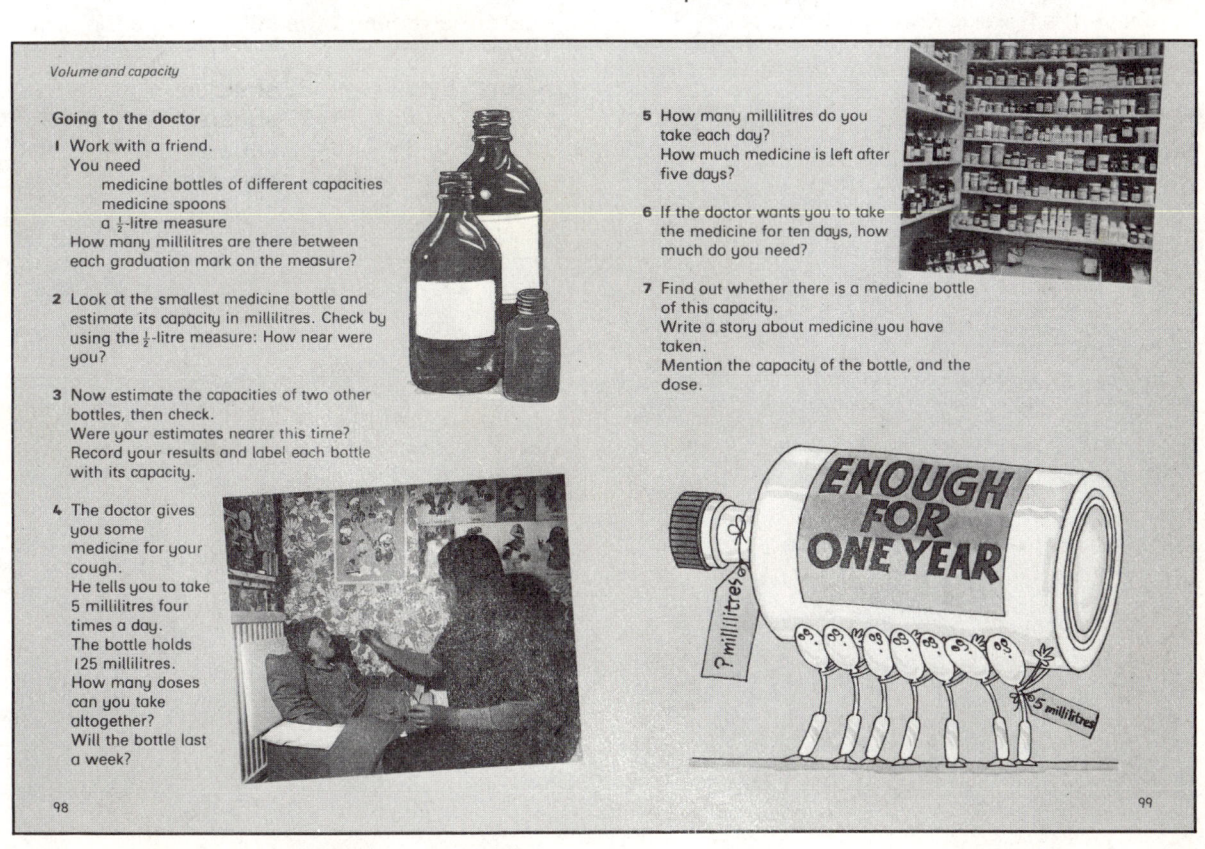

Volume and capacity

Going to the doctor

1 Work with a friend.
  You need
    medicine bottles of different capacities
    medicine spoons
    a $\frac{1}{2}$-litre measure
  How many millilitres are there between each graduation mark on the measure?

2 Look at the smallest medicine bottle and estimate its capacity in millilitres. Check by using the $\frac{1}{2}$-litre measure. How near were you?

3 Now estimate the capacities of two other bottles, then check.
  Were your estimates nearer this time?
  Record your results and label each bottle with its capacity.

4 The doctor gives you some medicine for your cough.
  He tells you to take 5 millilitres four times a day.
  The bottle holds 125 millilitres.
  How many doses can you take altogether?
  Will the bottle last a week?

5 How many millilitres do you take each day?
  How much medicine is left after five days?

6 If the doctor wants you to take the medicine for ten days, how much do you need?

7 Find out whether there is a medicine bottle of this capacity.
  Write a story about medicine you have taken.
  Mention the capacity of the bottle, and the dose.

59

4. *Extend* by varying the dosage and the capacity of the medicine bottle.

Q4 25 doses; no

Q5 20 ml; 25 ml

Q6 200 ml

Page 100 Checkpoint

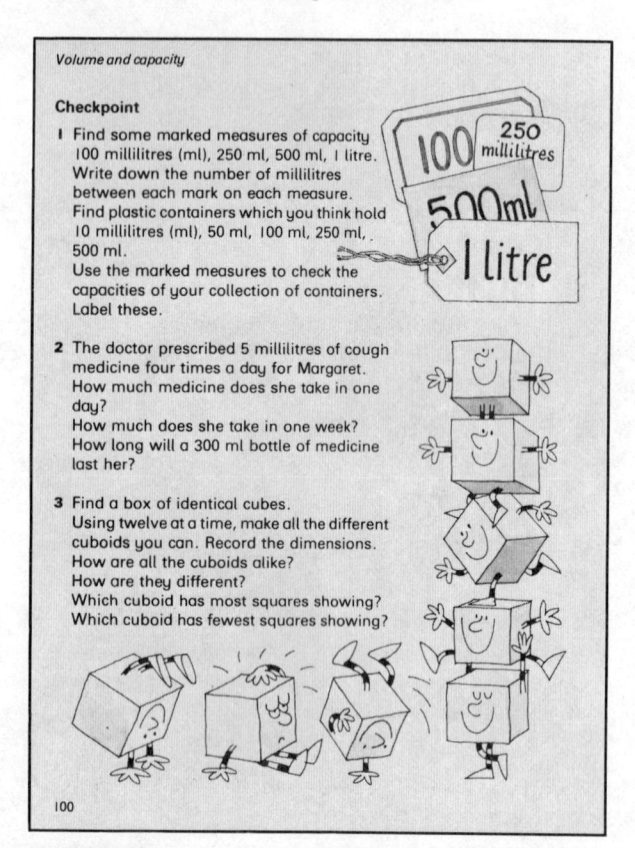

Volume and capacity

Checkpoint

1 Find some marked measures of capacity 100 millilitres (ml), 250 ml, 500 ml, 1 litre. Write down the number of millilitres between each mark on each measure. Find plastic containers which you think hold 10 millilitres (ml), 50 ml, 100 ml, 250 ml, 500 ml.
Use the marked measures to check the capacities of your collection of containers. Label these.

2 The doctor prescribed 5 millilitres of cough medicine four times a day for Margaret.
How much medicine does she take in one day?
How much does she take in one week?
How long will a 300 ml bottle of medicine last her?

3 Find a box of identical cubes.
Using twelve at a time, make all the different cuboids you can. Record the dimensions.
How are all the cuboids alike?
How are they different?
Which cuboid has most squares showing?
Which cuboid has fewest squares showing?

Content

Checking that the children can (a) estimate contents in millilitres; (b) use graduated containers to check capacities; (c) apply their knowledge of millilitres to problems; (d) make cuboids using identical cubes, and compare their surface areas.

Vocabulary

prescribe

Equipment

nest of graduated containers to 1 litre, unmarked containers of capacity 10 ml (bottle top), 50 ml, 100 ml, 250 ml, 500 ml and 1 litre, identical cubes

Notes

Q1 If a child cannot find an unmarked container of capacity, say, 250 ml, ask him or her to find a container which is nearest in capacity to 250 ml.

Q2 The medicine will last 15 days.

Q3 The dimensions of the cuboids (in cubic centimetres) and the surface area (sq cm) are:

    1 by 1 by 12 ⟶ 50 squares
    2 by 2 by 3   ⟶ 32 squares
    1 by 2 by 6   ⟶ 40 squares
    1 by 3 by 4   ⟶ 38 squares

The volumes are all 12 cubes.

Number

Pages 101 and 102 What is your perimeter?

Content
Finding body measurements, recording these in decimetres and centimetres, and as decimals of a decimetre.
Arranging lengths in order.
Finding the differences between body measurements; recording these as decimals of decimetres.

Equipment
centimetre squared paper, crayons or paints, perimeter strips of different colours

Notes
1. Each child within a group should choose one colour for all his strips.
2. Children require much practice in writing their own measures in decimetres and centimetres and as decimals of a decimetre. Give short daily practice and ask them to measure their finger perimeters, finger lengths, crowns, etc. Sometimes give simple conversions, eg write 3 dm 5 cm as a decimal of a decimetre.
3. The children should keep their own strips for later work.
4. Discuss with the children the two methods of subtraction.

    (a) Shopkeeper's method (see diagram) In some cases this method of adding on is more easily understood by the children as they compare the lengths.

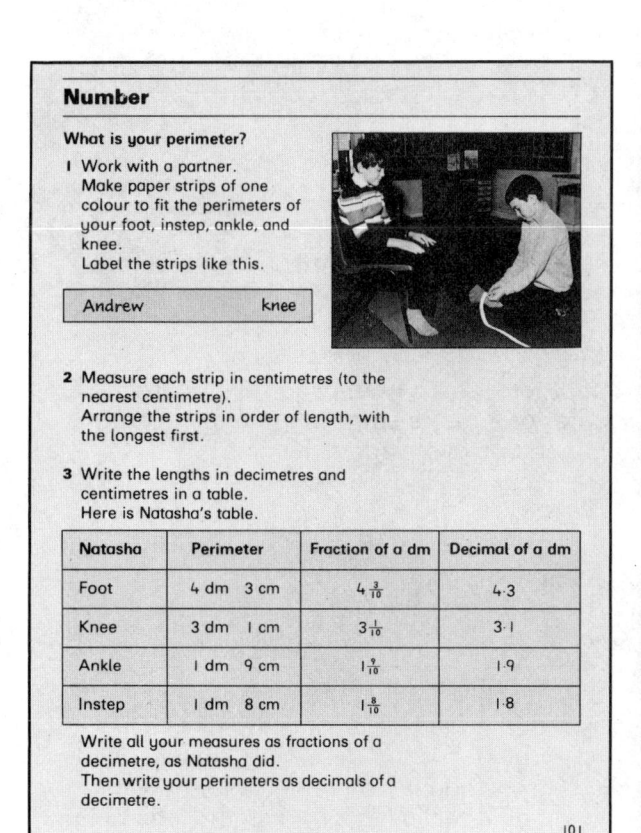

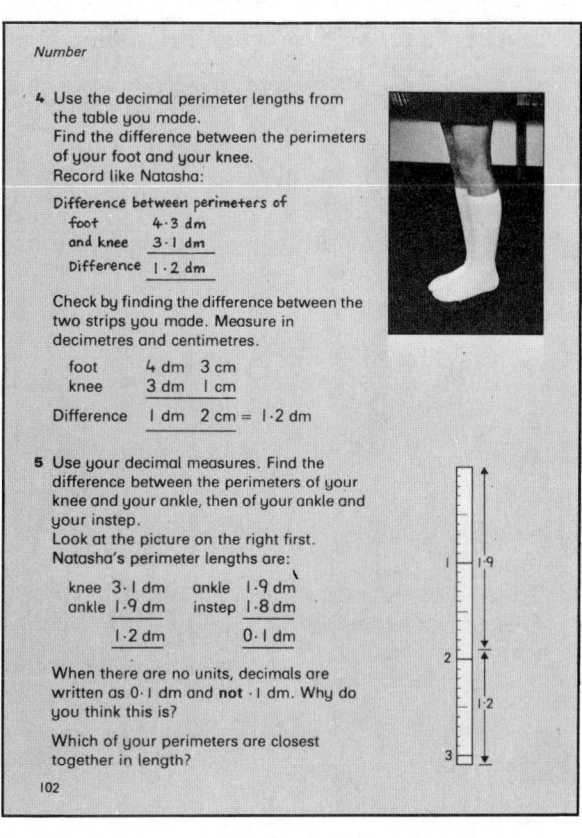

Number

What is your perimeter?

1. Work with a partner.
Make paper strips of one colour to fit the perimeters of your foot, instep, ankle, and knee.
Label the strips like this.

Andrew	knee

2. Measure each strip in centimetres (to the nearest centimetre).
Arrange the strips in order of length, with the longest first.

3. Write the lengths in decimetres and centimetres in a table.
Here is Natasha's table.

Natasha	Perimeter	Fraction of a dm	Decimal of a dm
Foot	4 dm 3 cm	$4\frac{3}{10}$	4·3
Knee	3 dm 1 cm	$3\frac{1}{10}$	3·1
Ankle	1 dm 9 cm	$1\frac{9}{10}$	1·9
Instep	1 dm 8 cm	$1\frac{8}{10}$	1·8

Write all your measures as fractions of a decimetre, as Natasha did.
Then write your perimeters as decimals of a decimetre.

101

Number

4. Use the decimal perimeter lengths from the table you made.
Find the difference between the perimeters of your foot and your knee.
Record like Natasha:

Difference between perimeters of
foot   4·3 dm
and knee 3·1 dm
Difference 1·2 dm

Check by finding the difference between the two strips you made. Measure in decimetres and centimetres.

foot	4 dm 3 cm
knee	3 dm 1 cm
Difference	1 dm 2 cm = 1·2 dm

5. Use your decimal measures. Find the difference between the perimeters of your knee and your ankle, then of your ankle and your instep.
Look at the picture on the right first.
Natasha's perimeter lengths are:

knee 3·1 dm   ankle 1·9 dm
ankle 1·9 dm   instep 1·8 dm
―――――――   ―――――――
1·2 dm   0·1 dm

When there are no units, decimals are written as 0·1 dm and **not** ·1 dm. Why do you think this is?

Which of your perimeters are closest together in length?

102

61

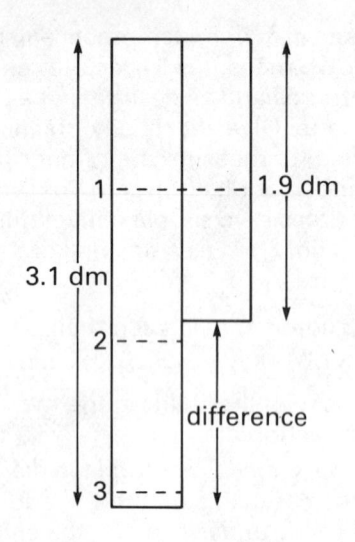

[Diagram: rectangle showing 3.1 dm total with 1.9 dm section and "difference" marked between levels 2 and 3]

(b) Decomposition method
  3 dm 1 cm ⟶ 2 dm 11 cm
 −1 dm 9 cm ⟶ 1 dm   9 cm
              1 dm   2 cm   1.2 dm

5. The children will need short daily practice, eg 'Find the difference between 4.5 cm and 1.8 cm, etc.

6. *Extend* by including other measures.

Worksheet 21 provides further estimating and measuring work.

Answers

2 (a) 1.8 dm (b) 1.2 dm (c) 2.2 dm
    (d) 1.2 dm

Worksheet 22 provides extra work with number patterns and decimals.

Answers

1 (a) 8 16 24 32   (b) 12 20 28 36
         \ / \ / \ /   \ / \ / \ /
          8   8   8   8   8   8

2 3 5 7 9 11 13 15 17 19
      \/ \/ \/ \/ \/ \/ \/ \/
       2 2 2 2   2   2   2   2

3 Aruna finds the ice-cream (add on 0.2 each time)
John finds the banana (add on 0.3 each time)
Emma finds the marbles (add on 0.4 each time)

Page 103 More about decimals

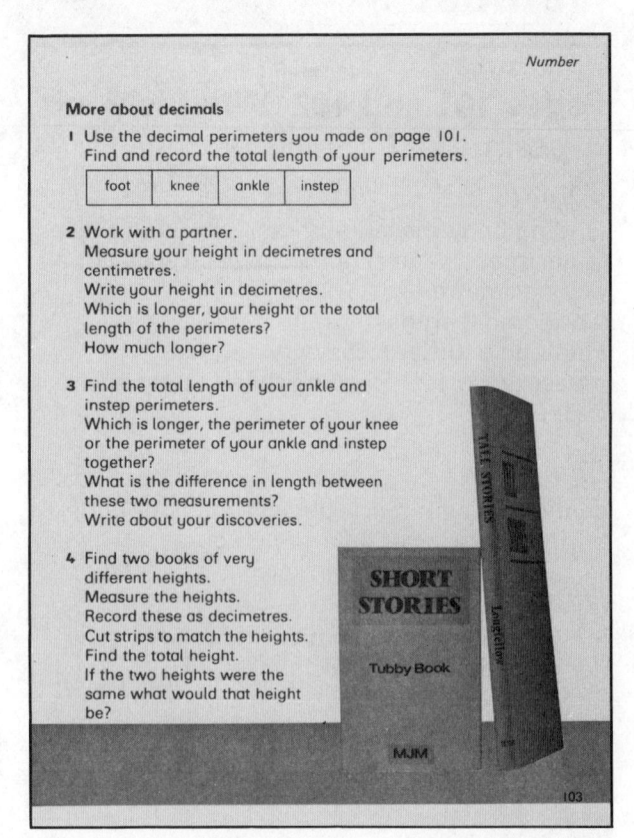

Number

More about decimals

1 Use the decimal perimeters you made on page 101.
Find and record the total length of your perimeters.

| foot | knee | ankle | instep |

2 Work with a partner.
Measure your height in decimetres and centimetres.
Write your height in decimetres.
Which is longer, your height or the total length of the perimeters?
How much longer?

3 Find the total length of your ankle and instep perimeters.
Which is longer, the perimeter of your knee or the perimeter of your ankle and instep together?
What is the difference in length between these two measurements?
Write about your discoveries.

4 Find two books of very different heights.
Measure the heights.
Record these as decimetres.
Cut strips to match the heights.
Find the total height.
If the two heights were the same what would that height be?

Content
More decimals using body measurements; adding and subtracting decimal lengths.

Equipment
perimeter strips from page 101, height measurer or 2-metre strip, centimetre squared paper, books of various heights

Notes
Remind the children how to record dm/cm as a decimal of 1 dm.

Q2 A 2-metre strip (on centimetre squared paper) can be fixed to the wall.

Q4 The children first find the total height by adding the two heights together. They should check by fastening the two height strips together end to end. By now they should realise that folding the long height strip will solve the problem. Repeat this with four books of different heights.

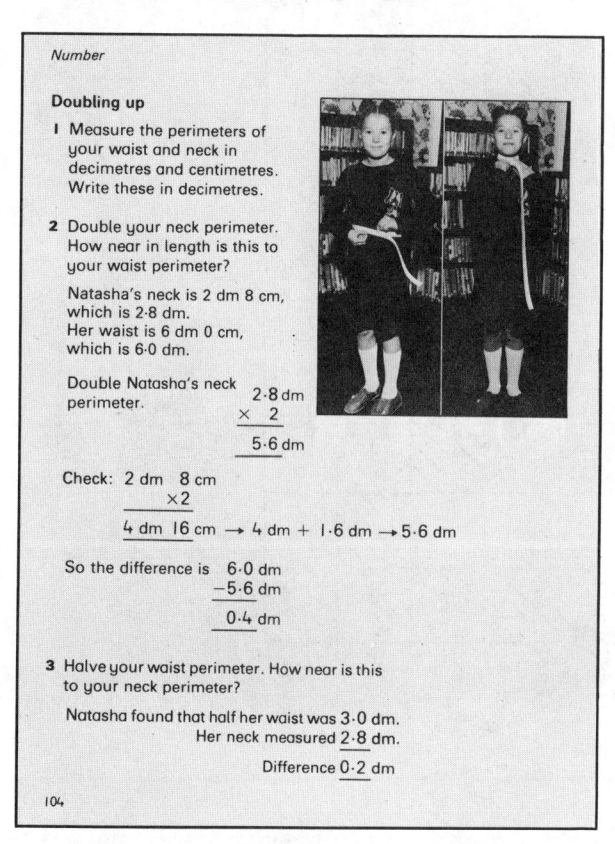

Page 104 Doubling up

> **Number**
>
> **Doubling up**
>
> 1. Measure the perimeters of your waist and neck in decimetres and centimetres. Write these in decimetres.
>
> 2. Double your neck perimeter. How near in length is this to your waist perimeter?
>
> Natasha's neck is 2 dm 8 cm, which is 2·8 dm.
> Her waist is 6 dm 0 cm, which is 6·0 dm.
>
> Double Natasha's neck perimeter.
> $$\begin{array}{r} 2\cdot8 \text{ dm} \\ \times\ 2 \\ \hline 5\cdot6 \text{ dm} \end{array}$$
>
> Check: $\begin{array}{r} 2 \text{ dm } 8 \text{ cm} \\ \times 2 \\ \hline 4 \text{ dm } 16 \text{ cm} \end{array}$ → 4 dm + 1·6 dm → 5·6 dm
>
> So the difference is $\begin{array}{r} 6\cdot0 \text{ dm} \\ -5\cdot6 \text{ dm} \\ \hline 0\cdot4 \text{ dm} \end{array}$
>
> 3. Halve your waist perimeter. How near is this to your neck perimeter?
>
> Natasha found that half her waist was 3·0 dm.
> Her neck measured 2·8 dm.
> Difference 0·2 dm

Content
Multiplication and division using decimals.

Equipment
perimeter strips, centimetre squared paper

Notes
1. Discuss with the children the fact that working in decimetres/centimetres gives the same answer as when using decimals of a decimetre.
2. Check that the same results can be obtained by doubling or halving the perimeter strips.
3. *Extend* by using other body measurements, eg compare four times the wrist with the waist; compare twice the waist with the height.

Worksheet 23 gives practice and extension of work with decimals.

Answers
1. The shape made is a 5-pointed star.
2. 4.5, 4.6, 4.7, 4.8, 4.9, 5.0, 5.1, 5.2, 5.3, 5.4, 5.5, 5.6, 5.7
3. (a) 3.9 (b) 4.7 (c) 5.9 (d) 3.1 (e) 5.1
4. (a) 5.4 dm (b) 7.2 dm (c) 3 dm (d) 5.6 dm (e) 9.8 dm

Page 105 Practice page

> **Number**
>
> **Practice page**
>
> | 1. 26 + 12 | 2. 42 + 29 | 3. 20 + 30 | 4. 46 + 8 |
> |---|---|---|---|
> | 5. 46 − 3 | 6. 60 − 20 | 7. 51 − 8 | 8. 70 − 24 |
>
> 9. Multiply each of these numbers by 4. (a) 6 (b) 7 (c) 9 (d) 14
>
> | 10. 23 × 8 | 11. 24 × 6 | 12. 26 × 5 | 13. 23 × 9 |
> |---|---|---|---|
>
> 14. Biscuits cost 36p a packet. How much would six packets cost?
>
> 15. A ferry boat crosses a river 24 times a day. How many crossings does it make in five days?
>
> 16. 44 ÷ 3   17. 93 ÷ 7   18. 120 ÷ 10   19. 83 ÷ 5
>
> 20. Caroline chooses some Christmas cards which cost 6p each. How many could she buy for (a) 50p, (b) £1, (c) £2?
>
> 21. A piece of construction kit is 3 centimetres long. How many pieces would be needed to make
>   (a) 1 metre,
>   (b) 1 metre 50 centimetres,
>   (c) 2 metres?
>
> 22. A can of drink costs 18p. How many cans could you buy for (a) £1, (b) £3, (c) £5?

Content
Addition and subtraction practice using 1-digit and 2-digit numbers. Multiplication and division practice.

Equipment
ten-sticks and units, number lines

Notes
1. Precede by giving the children practice with expanded notation, eg 51 → 50 + 1 → 40 + 11, etc, and reminding them of the methods of subtraction: (a) shopkeeper's, (b) decomposition.

2. Discuss with the children multiplication of a 2-digit number by a 1-digit number,

eg   23 ⟶ 20 + 3
      × 3   × 3
                 60 + 9 ⟶ 69

3. Discuss the method of division by repeated subtraction and ask the children to check their answers.

4. Some children will need further practice. Question them from time to time to ensure understanding, eg ask a child to work aloud.

Q1 38   Q2 71   Q3 50   Q4 54
Q5   43   Q6 40   Q7 43   Q8 46
Q9 (a) 24   (b) 28   (c) 36   (d) 56
Q10 184   Q11 144   Q12 130 Q13 207
Q14 £2.16   Q15 120 crossings
Q16 14 and 2 left   Q17 13 and 2 left
Q18 12   Q19 16 and 3 left
Q20 (a) 8   (b) 16   (c) 33
Q21 (a) 34   (b) 50   (c) 67
Q22 (a) 5   (b) 16   (c) 27

Worksheet 24 provides further division practice in the form of number-crosses.

Answers

1

a 2	4		b 2
1		c 2	3
	d 2	6	
e 1	3		

2

a 1	5		b 1
4		c 2	6
	d 1	7	
e 4	1		

3

a 3	5		b 1
1		c 1	6
d 2	e 2		6
	f 3	4	

64

Mass

Page 106 Does it balance?

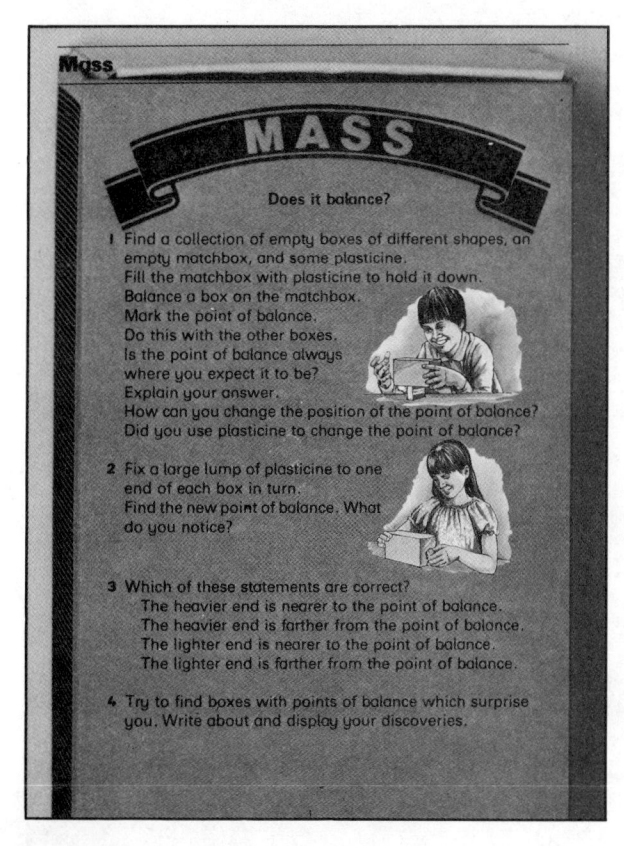

Content
Finding the point of balance of objects of different shapes.

Vocabulary
point of balance

Equipment
empty boxes of different shapes, empty matchboxes, plasticine

Notes
Q1 The children will find long boxes easier to balance at first. Ask the children to mark the point of balance on each object. The position of the point of balance can depend on the way in which the box is constructed ie with flaps.

Q2 When plasticine is added to the boxes, ask the children why the point of balance is not where it was.

Q3 This represents an inverse relation. The heavier end is nearer to the point of balance (ie distance is less).

Extend by asking the children to find the point of balance of various card shapes. Some children will do this by balancing the shape on the unsharpened end of a pencil. Include both regular and irregular shapes.

Page 107 Balance the broom

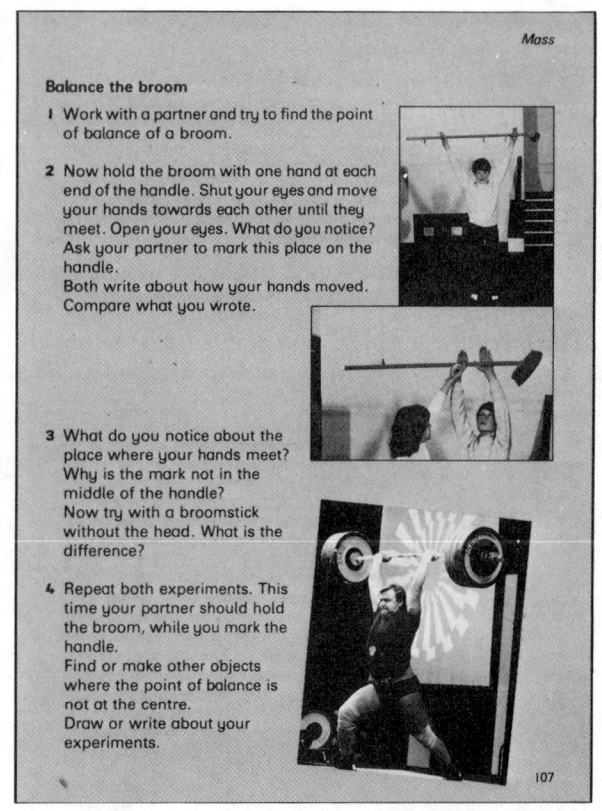

Content
Finding the point of balance of a broomstick.

Equipment
brooms and mops, broomsticks, plasticine, metre sticks, string, sheets of card

Notes
1. The children should experiment with brooms and mops of different lengths, as well as with broomsticks.

Add a large lump of plasticine to one end of a metre stick. Distances from the point of balance can be compared by using string.

2. *Applications*

(a) Robin Hood project – making arrows for a bow.
The children can find the point of balance of arrows and compare the flight of arrows in which the point of balance is in different positions.

(b) Making a wind arrow from two sheets of card.
Cut two identical arrows.
The axis should be left open when the two arrows are stuck together.
An empty pen top is fixed in the gap. The pen top is balanced on a ballpoint pen to allow the arrow to rotate (see figure).

Q2 Try this experiment yourself first. The hands move at different rates. The children's descriptions should show whether they understand this. Ask them which hand moves first and why this happens.

Q3 Precede by questioning the children about the position of the end with greater mass. Is this nearer to or farther from the point of balance than the other end?
Also question them about the end with less mass. Ask them to complete the statements:

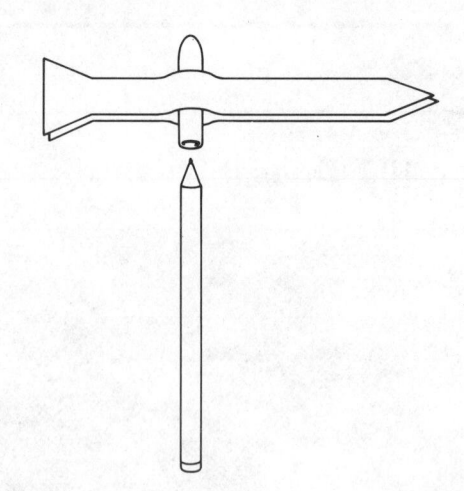

The greater the mass the .... its distance from the point of balance.

The less the mass the .... its distance from the point of balance.

Pages 108 and 109 Cooking time

Mass

Cooking time

1 Find three identical yoghurt pots.
Check on balance scales.
Fill one pot to the brim with sugar. Fill another to the brim with flour. Do the pots still balance one another?
Fill the third yoghurt pot with flour. Do the two pots of flour balance the pot of sugar? What does this tell you about sugar and flour?

2 Weigh out the ingredients to make Oat Crunch biscuits.
What is the total mass of the ingredients?

Oats 220 grams
Margarine 200 grams
Sugar 150 grams

Melt the margarine in a tin (you could do this on a hot, wide-topped radiator).
Mix the oats and sugar in a bowl.
Pour the melted margarine into the mixture.
Mix well.
Find the total mass of the mixture.
Is this the same as the total mass of the ingredients?
Roll the mixture into balls as big as a walnut shell.
Put the balls into a baking tin, leaving spaces in between.
Flatten them a little: Cook for 15 minutes (oven mark 5, 375°F).

Mass

3 When the biscuits are cooked, find the total mass.
Is this the same as before? If not, what is the difference in mass?

How many biscuits did you make altogether?
Find the mass of 10 biscuits.
Can you find the mass of one biscuit?
Do all the biscuits have the same mass?
How did you find out?

4 Put 200 g of flour into a plastic container.
Find something which has a mass of 200 g but has greater volume than the flour.
Then find another object which has a mass of 200 g but has less volume than the flour.

Content
Comparing masses of the same volume of flour and sugar. Using cooking to give practice in weighing quantities.

Equipment
identical yoghurt pots, balance scales, flour, sugar, ingredients for recipe (oats, margarine, sugar), bowls and tins for cooking, baking sheets or tins, plastic containers, various objects with mass of 200 g (polystyrene, plasticine, etc)

Notes
1. At this stage, it is better for the children to use balance scales and standard masses to measure out the ingredients.
2. If there is no oven available in your school, there is usually an oven in the infant school.

Q1 The two pots full of flour should approximately balance one pot full of sugar.

Q2 If the children have measured out the masses accurately, the mass of the final mixture should be the same as that of all the ingredients.

Q3 During cooking, moisture is lost, so the cooked biscuits should have less mass than before cooking.
The best way to check whether all the biscuits have the same mass (this is unlikely) is to try to balance two different sets of 10 biscuits.

Q4 200 g of polystyrene pieces would have greater volume than flour. A 200 g mass or 200 g of water would have less volume than flour.

Page 110 Make a dart

Content
Experiments with points of balance using paper darts.

Vocabulary
point of balance

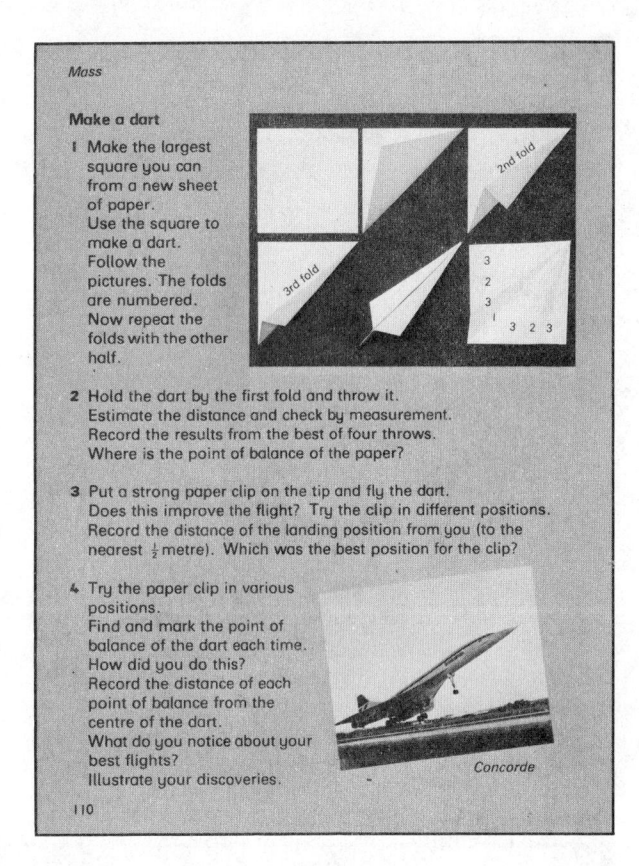

Equipment
sheets of paper, paper clips, string, bulldog clips

Notes
1. We suggest that you try this yourself first! The experiments should be done outside on a calm day.
2. The children could make string measures marked in metres (one colour) and half-metres (another colour).
3. The flight is best when the paper clip is nearest to the tip of the dart.
4. *Extend* by asking the children to use two clips or a bulldog clip. When two clips are used, they can be close together or in different positions.

67

Page 111 Checkpoint

Checkpoint

1. Make a ball of plasticine which you think has a mass of 200 g. Check, using balance scales. How near was your estimate? Make your ball into one which has a mass of 200 g.
Experiment to find an object with the same mass as your ball. Label it.

2. Halve your plasticine ball. Check to see whether each part has a mass of 100 g.
Now halve a 100 g mass.
Experiment to find an object with a mass of 100 g, and one with a mass of 50 g. Find another object with a 'net mass' of 100 g. What do you think 'net mass' means? Does your object have a mass of 100 g?

3. Find compression scales which have a maximum reading of 4 kg. Use these to find objects with masses of 1 kg, 2 kg, 3 kg.
Make a list, in order, of all the objects you tried, with their masses.

Content
Checking that the children understand the various concepts, and can use the appropriate language patterns. Providing extra practice in measuring masses.

Vocabulary
net mass, compression scales

Equipment
plasticine, balance scales, 200 g masses, objects with mass of 200 g, 100 g masses, 50 g masses, objects with masses of 100 g and 50 g, compression scales, objects with masses of 1 kg, 2 kg, 3 kg.

Notes

Q1 Make sure that there are one or two objects with a mass of 200 g or provide plastic bags, sand and fasteners so that masses can be made.

Q2 Observe whether the child includes all the plasticine from the 200 g ball in his experiment.
Make sure that objects with masses of 100 g and 50 g are available or can be made. Very few commodities are labelled 'net mass'. Packets are often incorrectly labelled 'net weight'. Discuss this problem with the children. Also ask them to look out for incorrect abbreviations of grams, etc. The correct abbreviation is g (by international agreement) not grms or gms.

Q3 Compression scales should have a maximum capacity of 5 kg. Suitable objects for this experiment are books, potatoes, large stones, or the children can use strong plastic bags and sand. The greater masses may be difficult to find.

Worksheet 25 provides some practice in calculations involving grams.

Answers

1. (a) 10 g (b) 15 g (c) 40 g
   (d) 65 g (e) 25 g (f) 90 g

2.
1	125 g	25p
2	250 g	50p
3	375 g	75p
4	500 g	£1.00
5	625 g	£1.25
10	1250 g	£2.50
15	1875 g	£3.75
20	2500 g	£5.00

Shape

Pages 112 and 113 Turning the tortoise

Content
Using a template to make (a) patterns with rotational symmetry, (b) patterns with mirror symmetry.

Vocabulary
template

Equipment
card for templates, scissors, sheets of plain paper, pins, paint and brushes, kaleidoscopes, hinged mirrors

Notes

1. The card should be pliable enough to cut with scissors but not too thin to use as a template.

2. The template has to be turned over to make a mirror image of the tortoise (in the upside-down pattern).

3. When the patterns have been made, they should be painted and displayed. Different colours should be used for mirror and rotational patterns.

4. It is because the tortoise template has no mirror symmetry that a pattern cannot be made with both mirror and rotational symmetry.

5. *Extend* by asking the children to make a unit pattern with mirror symmetry. Suggest that they use this as a template to make coloured patterns for display. The display could be accompanied by a written account. It would be useful to have some kaleidoscopes available and also hinged mirrors so that these could be used in pattern-making.

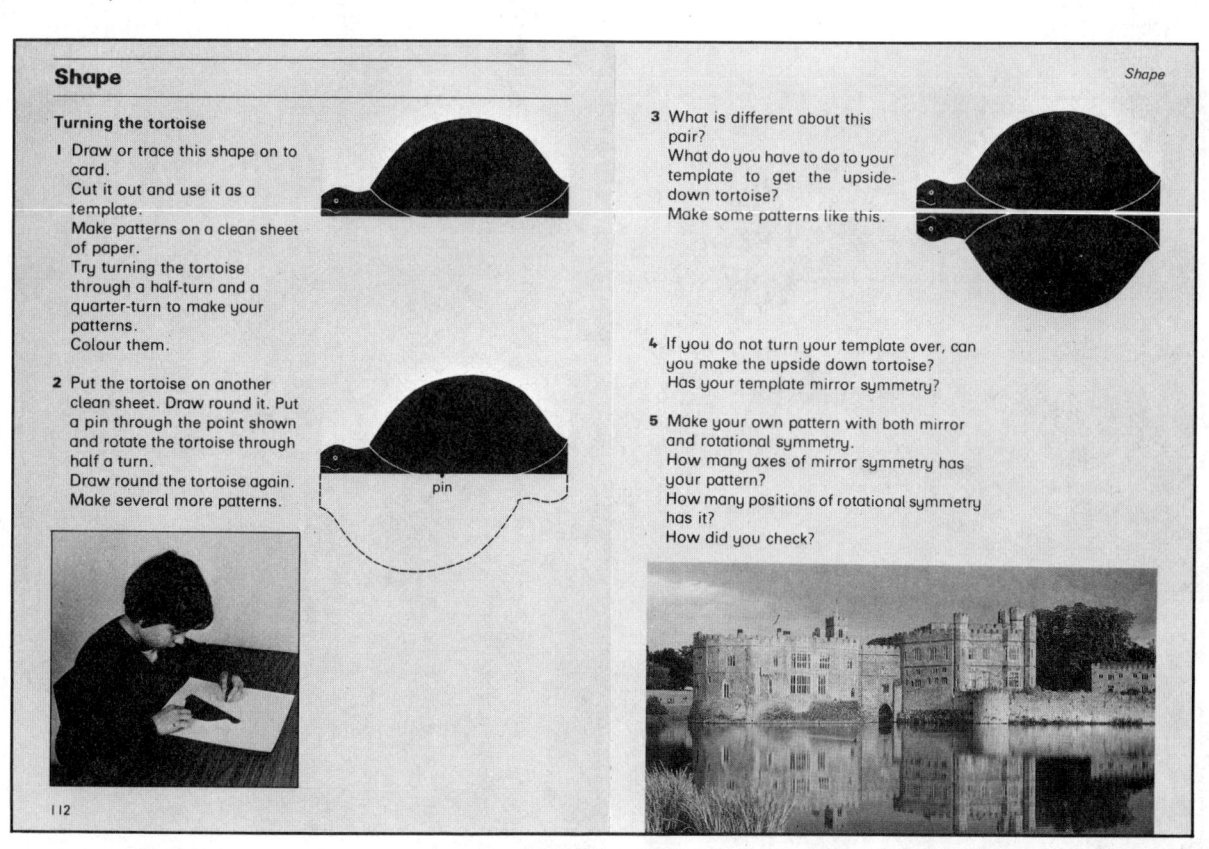

Shape

Turning the tortoise

1 Draw or trace this shape on to card.
Cut it out and use it as a template.
Make patterns on a clean sheet of paper.
Try turning the tortoise through a half-turn and a quarter-turn to make your patterns.
Colour them.

2 Put the tortoise on another clean sheet. Draw round it. Put a pin through the point shown and rotate the tortoise through half a turn.
Draw round the tortoise again.
Make several more patterns.

3 What is different about this pair?
What do you have to do to your template to get the upside-down tortoise?
Make some patterns like this.

4 If you do not turn your template over, can you make the upside down tortoise?
Has your template mirror symmetry?

5 Make your own pattern with both mirror and rotational symmetry.
How many axes of mirror symmetry has your pattern?
How many positions of rotational symmetry has it?
How did you check?

Pages 114 and 115 Checkpoint

Content
Checking whether the children can (a) make the largest square possible from a sheet of paper; (b) make shapes with matching edges and recognise whether these shapes have mirror or rotational symmetry, or both; (c) recognise that shapes can have the same area even though their perimeters are different; (d) understand the concept of enlargement (squares); (e) follow directions to make shapes; (f) compare areas made with different identical shapes; (g) find which shapes fit together without leaving gaps (tessellation).

Vocabulary
octagon, parallelogram, right-angled triangle, isosceles triangle (from a Greek word meaning 'equal legs'), centre of rotation, diamond

Equipment
plain paper, centimetre squared paper, rulers, scissors, coloured pencils, paint and brushes

Notes
1. Precede by checking that the children remember how to make the largest square from a sheet of paper. It would be useful to provide paper which has typing on one side to distinguish one side from the other.

Q1 The triangles of paper are right-angled and have two equal edges. Some children may be ready for the word 'isosceles'. One angle is a right-angle. Ask the children why this is (corners of the original square).

Q2 Three different shapes can be made.
(a) A square.

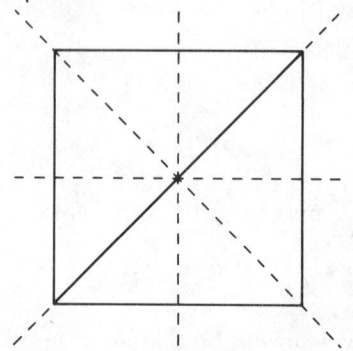

This has mirror symmetry and rotational symmetry. Ask the children to mark in the axes of mirror symmetry. Ask them to show the centre of rotation (point of turn).

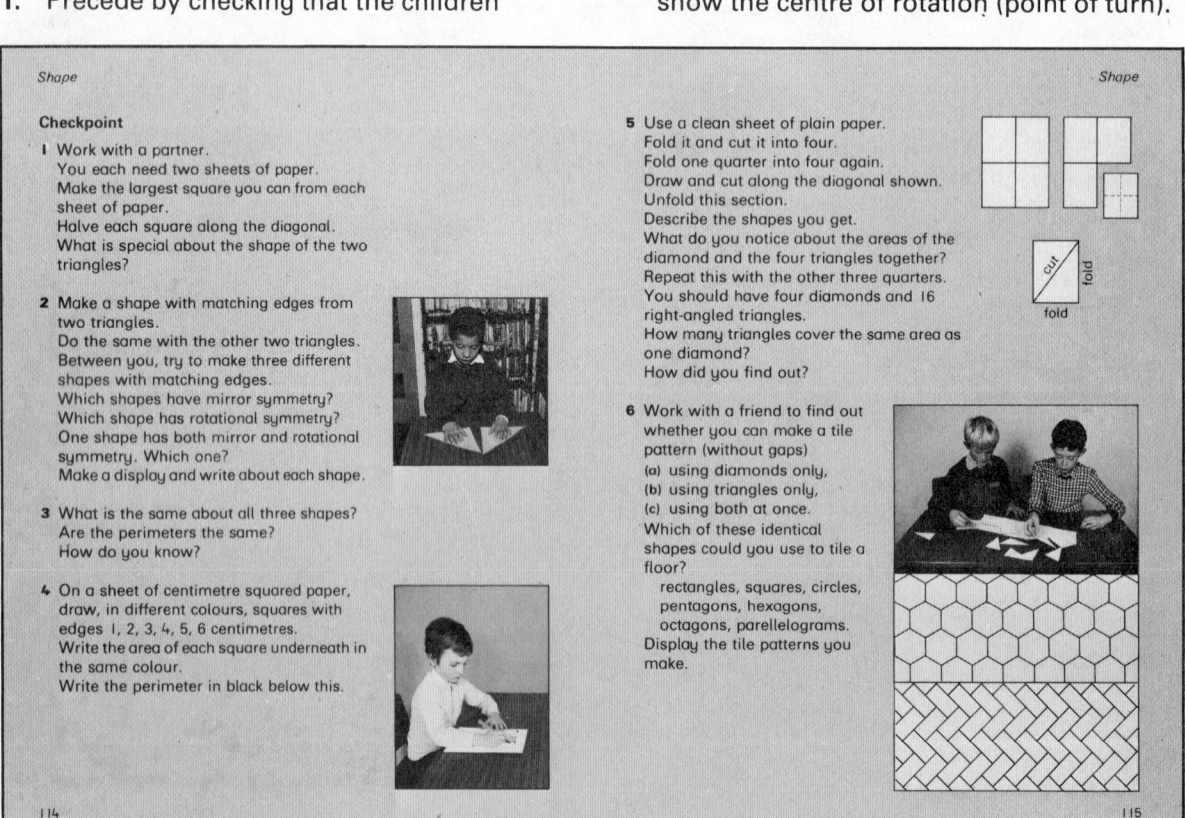

Shape

Checkpoint

1. Work with a partner.
   You each need two sheets of paper.
   Make the largest square you can from each sheet of paper.
   Halve each square along the diagonal.
   What is special about the shape of the two triangles?

2. Make a shape with matching edges from two triangles.
   Do the same with the other two triangles.
   Between you, try to make three different shapes with matching edges.
   Which shapes have mirror symmetry?
   Which shape has rotational symmetry?
   One shape has both mirror and rotational symmetry. Which one?
   Make a display and write about each shape.

3. What is the same about all three shapes?
   Are the perimeters the same?
   How do you know?

4. On a sheet of centimetre squared paper, draw, in different colours, squares with edges 1, 2, 3, 4, 5, 6 centimetres.
   Write the area of each square underneath in the same colour.
   Write the perimeter in black below this.

5. Use a clean sheet of plain paper.
   Fold it and cut it into four.
   Fold one quarter into four again.
   Draw and cut along the diagonal shown.
   Unfold this section.
   Describe the shapes you get.
   What do you notice about the areas of the diamond and the four triangles together?
   Repeat this with the other three quarters.
   You should have four diamonds and 16 right-angled triangles.
   How many triangles cover the same area as one diamond?
   How did you find out?

6. Work with a friend to find out whether you can make a tile pattern (without gaps)
   (a) using diamonds only,
   (b) using triangles only,
   (c) using both at once.
   Which of these identical shapes could you use to tile a floor?
   rectangles, squares, circles, pentagons, hexagons, octagons, parellelograms.
   Display the tile patterns you make.

70

(b) A parallelogram (two identical triangles).

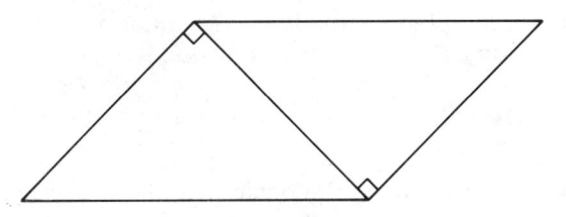

This has rotational symmetry.
Ask the children to mark the centre of rotation.

(c) A triangle.

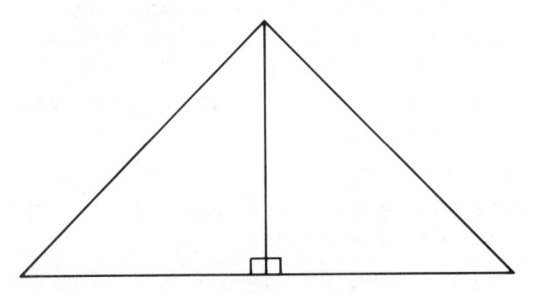

This is a triangle because its base is a straight line (two right-angles).
Ask the children how they know this.
It is an isosceles triangle (two equal edges).

Q3 The areas of all three shapes are the same. The perimeters are different.
Extend by asking the children to show the shapes with (a) the shortest perimeter, (b) the longest perimeter. Which two have the same perimeter?

Q4 The children will carry out this activity in different ways, eg overlapping squares, squares along a diagonal, or squares across the page.
All these are correct.

Q5 The children should finish with folds like this.

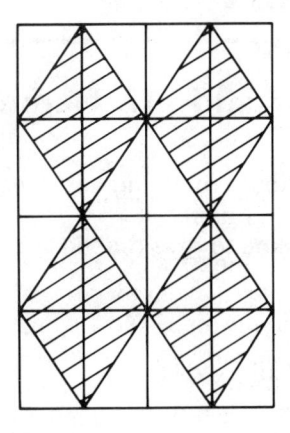

Four triangles have the same area as one diamond.
Some children will cut along the other diagonal. Ask them all to describe the shapes they get when this happens.

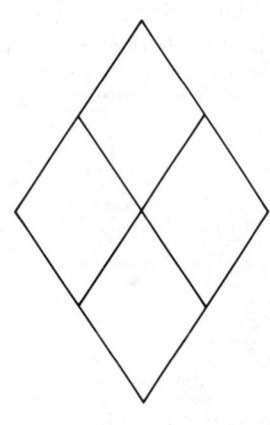

Q6 Suggest that each child uses a different colour to paint each set of diamonds. When the children have fitted four diamonds together ask: (a) Is the large diamond the same shape as the small one? (b) What is the ratio of the edges of the large and small diamonds? (c) Can you make a diamond whose edges are three times those of the small one? How many more small diamonds do you need to finish this?

Worksheet 26 can be used here to give extra practice in tessellating.

Number

Pages 116 and 117 Games

Content
Counting in fours (building and breaking a cube of edge 4 units).
A decimal game to give practice in adding decimals.

Equipment
interlocking cubes, dice

Notes

1. Check that the groups know the size of the cube being made or broken. Here it is a 4 by 4 by 4 cube.

2. As each child throws a die, listen to his partner's instructions. These should be precise. If for a score of 6, the partner says 'Take one stick and two units,' ask him to explain his instruction.

3. *Extend* by using cubes with other dimensions. When a 6 by 6 by 6 cube is used, it is better to provide two dice (and add the scores) before adding to, or subtracting from, the cube.

4. Before playing the decimal addition game, discuss with the children the fact that 10 tenths equal one unit.

5. Make sure that results are recorded each time.

6. Four throws is the least number of throws to score 20 or more. This could be reached with scores of 5 or more.
   Nineteen throws is the greatest number, if a score of 1.1 was scored each time.

7. *Extend* by starting with 20 and subtracting the score each time. The winner is the first to reach zero or below.

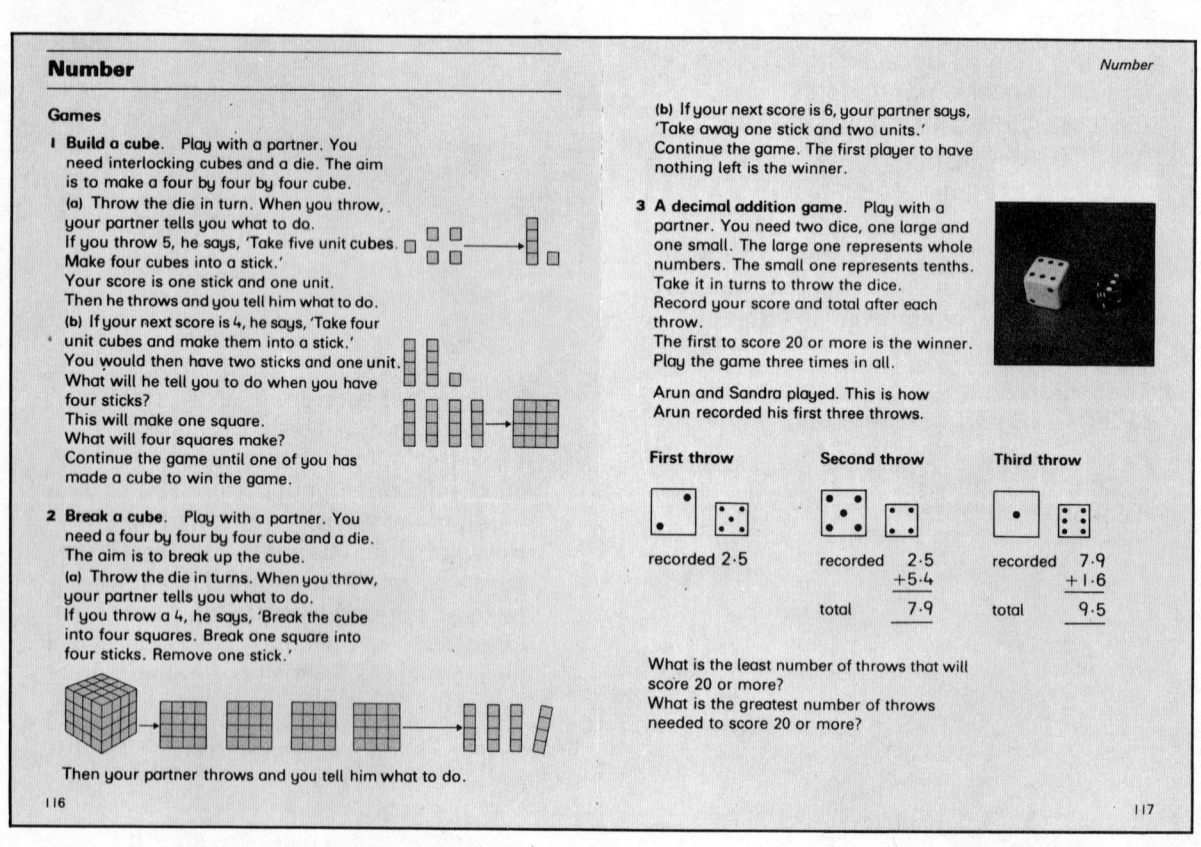

Number

Games

1 Build a cube. Play with a partner. You need interlocking cubes and a die. The aim is to make a four by four by four cube.
(a) Throw the die in turn. When you throw, your partner tells you what to do.
If you throw 5, he says, 'Take five unit cubes. Make four cubes into a stick.'
Your score is one stick and one unit.
Then he throws and you tell him what to do.
(b) If your next score is 4, he says, 'Take four unit cubes and make them into a stick.'
You would then have two sticks and one unit.
What will he tell you to do when you have four sticks?
This will make one square.
What will four squares make?
Continue the game until one of you has made a cube to win the game.

2 Break a cube. Play with a partner. You need a four by four by four cube and a die. The aim is to break up the cube.
(a) Throw the die in turns. When you throw, your partner tells you what to do.
If you throw a 4, he says, 'Break the cube into four squares. Break one square into four sticks. Remove one stick.'

Then your partner throws and you tell him what to do.

(b) If your next score is 6, your partner says, 'Take away one stick and two units.'
Continue the game. The first player to have nothing left is the winner.

3 A decimal addition game. Play with a partner. You need two dice, one large and one small. The large one represents whole numbers. The small one represents tenths.
Take it in turns to throw the dice.
Record your score and total after each throw.
The first to score 20 or more is the winner. Play the game three times in all.

Arun and Sandra played. This is how Arun recorded his first three throws.

First throw

recorded 2·5

Second throw

recorded 2·5
        +5·4
total   7·9

Third throw

recorded 7·9
        +1·6
total   9·5

What is the least number of throws that will score 20 or more?
What is the greatest number of throws needed to score 20 or more?

Page 118 Special numbers

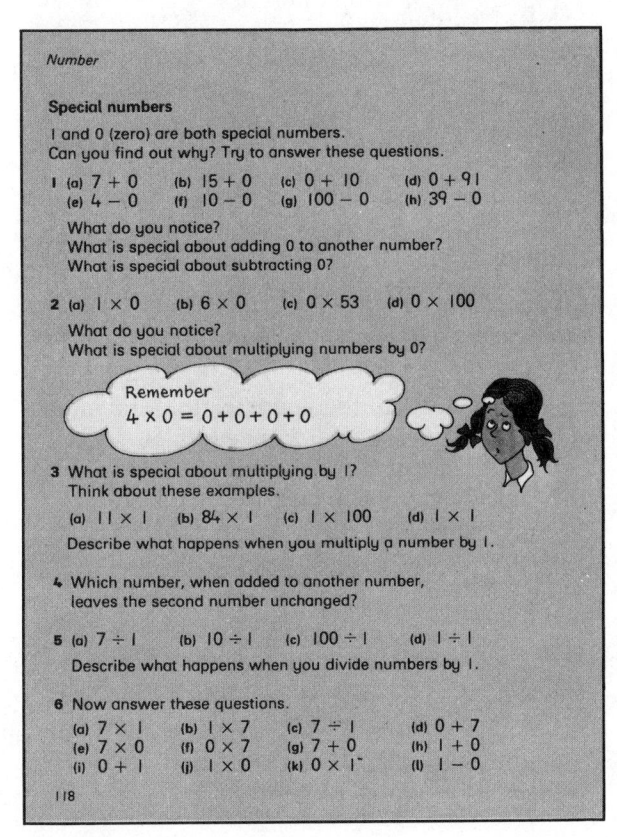

> *Number*
>
> **Special numbers**
>
> 1 and 0 (zero) are both special numbers.
> Can you find out why? Try to answer these questions.
>
> 1. (a) 7 + 0 (b) 15 + 0 (c) 0 + 10 (d) 0 + 91
>   (e) 4 − 0 (f) 10 − 0 (g) 100 − 0 (h) 39 − 0
>
>   What do you notice?
>   What is special about adding 0 to another number?
>   What is special about subtracting 0?
>
> 2. (a) 1 × 0 (b) 6 × 0 (c) 0 × 53 (d) 0 × 100
>
>   What do you notice?
>   What is special about multiplying numbers by 0?
>
> *Remember*
> 4 × 0 = 0 + 0 + 0 + 0
>
> 3. What is special about multiplying by 1?
>   Think about these examples.
>
>   (a) 11 × 1 (b) 84 × 1 (c) 1 × 100 (d) 1 × 1
>
>   Describe what happens when you multiply a number by 1.
>
> 4. Which number, when added to another number, leaves the second number unchanged?
>
> 5. (a) 7 ÷ 1 (b) 10 ÷ 1 (c) 100 ÷ 1 (d) 1 ÷ 1
>
>   Describe what happens when you divide numbers by 1.
>
> 6. Now answer these questions.
>   (a) 7 × 1 (b) 1 × 7 (c) 7 ÷ 1 (d) 0 + 7
>   (e) 7 × 0 (f) 0 × 7 (g) 7 + 0 (h) 1 + 0
>   (i) 0 + 1 (j) 1 × 0 (k) 0 × 1 (l) 1 − 0
>
> 118

Content

Multiplying and dividing any number by 1.
Multiplying by zero, adding zero to any number, subtracting zero from any number.

Notes

1. 1 and 0 are both special numbers in the way they react on other numbers.

Q1 When 0 is added to or subtracted from a number, the number stays the same.

Q2 The answer is 0 each time. When a number is multiplied by 0, the answer is always 0.

Q3 When multiplying by 1, the number is unaffected.

Q4 Addition of 0 leaves the other number unchanged.

Q5 When dividing by 1, the number being divided stays the same.

Q6 (a) 7 (b) 7 (c) 7 (d) 7 (e) 0 (f) 0
    (g) 7 (h) 1 (i) 1 (j) 0 (k) 0 (l) 1

Page 119 Reversing digits

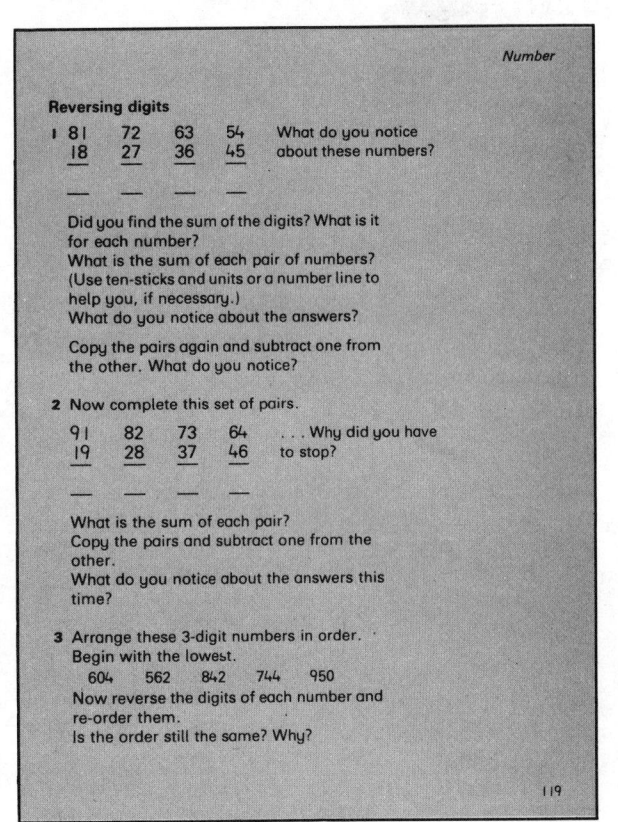

> *Number*
>
> **Reversing digits**
>
> 1. 81 72 63 54   What do you notice
>   18 27 36 45   about these numbers?
>   —   —   —   —
>
>   Did you find the sum of the digits? What is it for each number?
>   What is the sum of each pair of numbers?
>   (Use ten-sticks and units or a number line to help you, if necessary.)
>   What do you notice about the answers?
>
>   Copy the pairs again and subtract one from the other. What do you notice?
>
> 2. Now complete this set of pairs.
>
>   91 82 73 64   ... Why did you have
>   19 28 37 46   to stop?
>   —   —   —   —
>
>   What is the sum of each pair?
>   Copy the pairs and subtract one from the other.
>   What do you notice about the answers this time?
>
> 3. Arrange these 3-digit numbers in order. Begin with the lowest.
>   604   562   842   744   950
>   Now reverse the digits of each number and re-order them.
>   Is the order still the same? Why?
>
> 119

Content

Reversing 2-digit numbers and looking for patterns; reversing the numbers, adding or subtracting and looking for patterns.

Equipment

ten-sticks and units, number-line

Notes

Q1 Ask the children what they notice; be prepared for unexpected answers. They should notice that the numbers have been reversed. The digit sum is 9 in each case. The sums of the pairs are 99. The difference between each pair is divisible by 9.

Q2 The children have to stop the set because the next pair is 55
    55
    —

The sums of these pairs are all 110. When the children subtract they will get 72, 54, 36, 18. All answers are multiples of 9, and the digit sum of each answer is 9.

Q3 Some children will not be ready to work with 3-digits.
Order 562, 604, 744, 842, 950
The numbers with reversed digits are not in order. The order depends on the size of the units. When reversing 950, it becomes 095 which is 95.

Pages 120 and 121 Checkpoint

Content
Checking that the children (a) can recognise specific multiples and square numbers; (b) can carry out multiplication and division using money; (c) understand concepts of place value, simple fractions and decimal fractions.

Equipment
place value sheets, cards numbered 0 to 9, paper strips, centimetre squared paper, coloured pencils

Notes
Q1 (a) highest 919, lowest 151
(b) 265, 853, 151, 919
(c) 360
(d) 265, 360
(e) 360
(f) The digit sum of 7 occurs four times.

Q2 He spends £5.16. Change: £4.84.

Q3 14 litres (and just over $\frac{1}{4}$ litre).

Q4 Division by 2:
(a) 6, 8, 18
(b) 9, 13, 19
Division by 3:
(a) 6, 9, 18
(b) 13, 19

Q5 1, 4, 9, 16, 25 are square numbers.
1, 9, 25 are odd.

Q6 Make sure that the children do not change the position of a card once it is placed on the sheet. After each game the cards should not be replaced in the pack. Some children may be interested in finding the highest possible and lowest possible numbers (and scores). There are several solutions.

Q7 Provide paper strips to use for folding.
(a) $\frac{1}{2}$ (b) $\frac{3}{4}$ (c) $1\frac{1}{4}$ (d) 1 (e) $\frac{1}{2}$ (f) $\frac{3}{4}$ (g) $1\frac{1}{4}$
(h) $\frac{1}{4}$

Q8 (a) 0.8 (b) 0.2 (c) 1 (d) 0.4
These should be illustrated by the strips.

Number

Checkpoint

1 Here are 10 car numbers.

| 188 | 394 | 265 | 853 | 512 |
| 718 | 360 | 604 | 151 | 919 |

(a) Which is the highest number?
Which is the lowest number?
(b) Which numbers are odd?
(c) Which number is a multiple of 10?
(d) Which numbers are multiples of 5?
(e) Add the digits of each number until you get a single digit.
Which number is a multiple of 9?
(f) Which digit sum occurs most often?

2 Paul's father buys 12 litres of petrol at 43p a litre. How much change will he get from £10?

3 John's father spends £6 on petrol at 42p a litre. How many complete litres does he buy?

4 Which of these numbers, when divided by 2, have (a) no remainder, (b) remainder 1?
6   8   9   13   18   19
Repeat for division by 3.

5 Which of these are square numbers?
24   25   4   6   16   20   1   10   9
Write the square numbers in order.
Which of the square numbers are odd?

6 Make a place value sheet like this.
Use a pack of ten cards numbered 0 to 9.
Put the pack face down.
You are going to make the highest number you can with three cards.
Take one card. Decide where to put it.
Take a second card and put it in another column.
Now take a third card and put it in the empty column.
What is your number? Score 1 point for each 100. Was your number the highest possible?
Repeat this twice more with the cards that are left.
What is your total score?
Play again.
This time try to make the lowest number each time.

100	10	1

7 Work these. Use paper strips, folded in halves and quarters, if you need them.
(a) $\frac{1}{4} + \frac{1}{4}$ (b) $\frac{1}{2} + \frac{1}{4}$ (c) $\frac{3}{4} + \frac{1}{2}$ (d) $\frac{1}{2} + \frac{1}{2}$
(e) $1 - \frac{1}{2}$ (f) $1 - \frac{1}{4}$ (g) $2 - \frac{3}{4}$ (h) $1 - \frac{3}{4}$

8 Cut four strips, 10 cm long and 1 cm wide, from centimetre squared paper.
Use one strip to answer each of these (use colour to help).
(a) 0.5 + 0.3 (b) 0.5 − 0.3
(c) Double 0.5 (d) Half of 0.8

0·5	

Area

Pages 122 and 123 Checkpoint

Content
Checking that the children can find the areas and perimeters of shapes drawn on squared paper.

Equipment
centimetre squared paper, coloured pencils

Notes

Q1 (a) Make sure that the children have doubled all the dimensions of Jerry's garden, otherwise the two gardens will not be the same shape.

(b) The area of Jerry's garden is 4 sq m.
The area of Tom's garden is 16 sq m.
The ratio is
$$\frac{\text{Area of Tom's garden}}{\text{Area of Jerry's garden}} = \frac{16}{4} = \frac{4}{1}$$

(c) The perimeter of Jerry's garden is 10 m.
The perimeter of Tom's garden is 20 m.
The children can find this by counting or by using string.

Q2 The area of the square is 36 sq cm.
The area of the rectangle is 11 sq cm.
The area of the square is more than three times that of the rectangle.

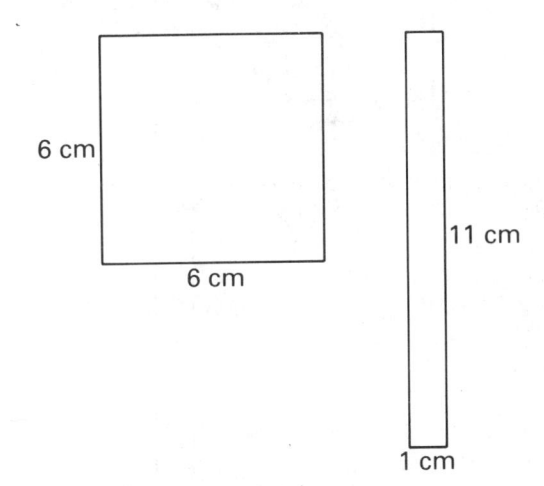

Q3 The perimeter of the square is 16 cm.
The perimeter of the rectangle is 34 cm.
The perimeter of the rectangle is more than double that of the square.
The difference between the perimeters is 18 cm.

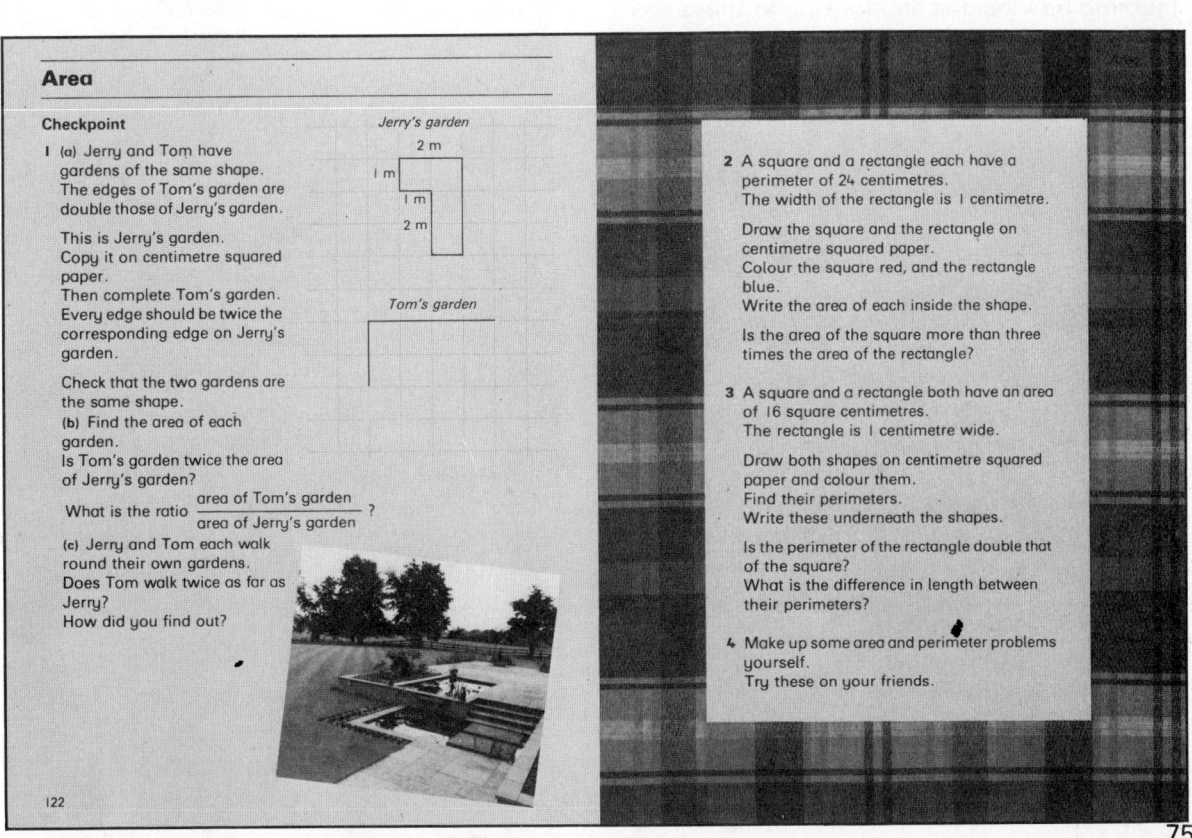

If the children colour their work, the shapes stand out and make a more attractive display.

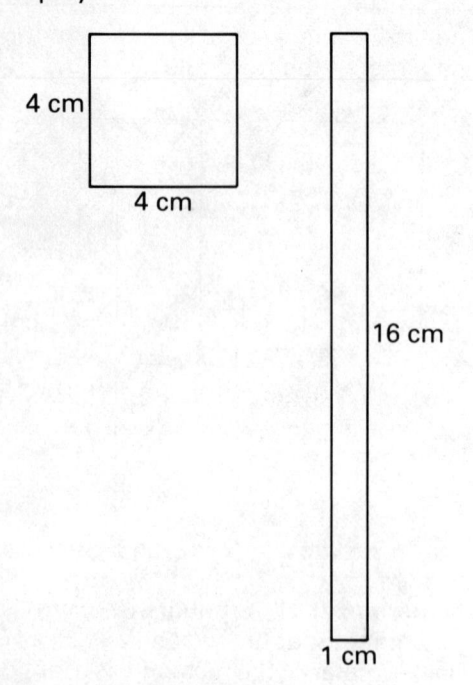

4 cm

4 cm

16 cm

1 cm

Q4 provides further practice.

Worksheet 27 gives additional practice in doubling dimensions and looking at the ratios of areas.

Time

Page 124 How long do you sleep?

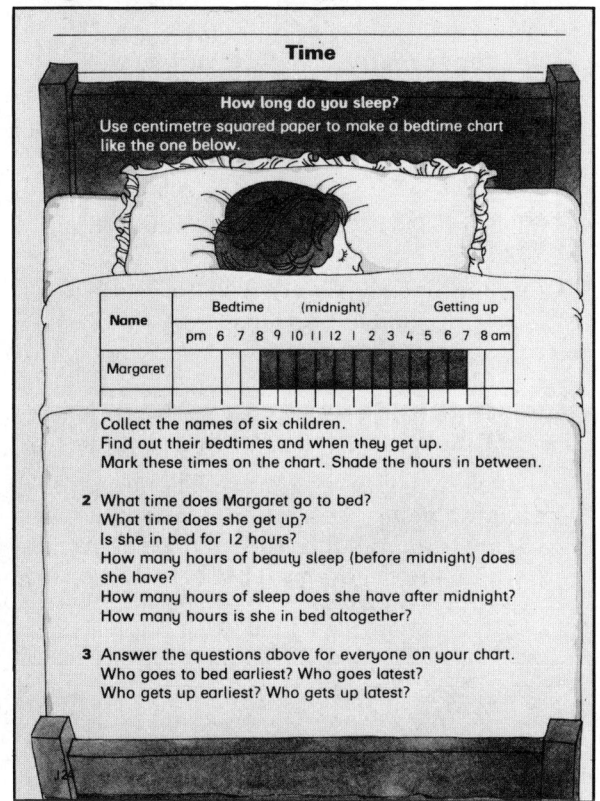

(Textbook page reproduction)

Time

How long do you sleep?
Use centimetre squared paper to make a bedtime chart like the one below.

Name	Bedtime						(midnight)					Getting up				
	pm 6	7	8	9	10	11	12	1	2	3	4	5	6	7	8 am
Margaret				■	■	■	■	■	■	■	■	■	■			

Collect the names of six children.
Find out their bedtimes and when they get up.
Mark these times on the chart. Shade the hours in between.

2 What time does Margaret go to bed?
What time does she get up?
Is she in bed for 12 hours?
How many hours of beauty sleep (before midnight) does she have?
How many hours of sleep does she have after midnight?
How many hours is she in bed altogether?

3 Answer the questions above for everyone on your chart.
Who goes to bed earliest? Who goes latest?
Who gets up earliest? Who gets up latest?

Content
Finding out how long children spend in bed (duration of time spanning midnight).

Equipment
centimetre squared paper

Notes
1. Precede by asking the children, on a particular night, to write the times they go to bed and get up (to the nearest hour). You may like to make your own class chart too. Hours should be written *on* the lines and not in the spaces, to avoid confusion.

2. Ask, 'Who was in bed the longest time? Who was in bed the shortest time? Were any children in bed for the same length of time? Did they go to bed at the same time?'

3. Ask the children to make up their own problems using the information in the chart.

Page 125 Introducing the 24-hour clock

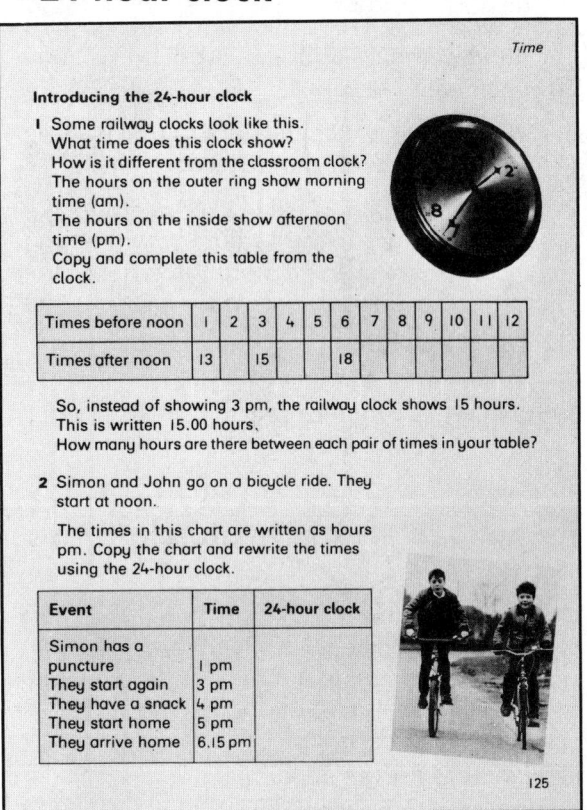

(Textbook page reproduction)

Introducing the 24-hour clock

1 Some railway clocks look like this.
What time does this clock show?
How is it different from the classroom clock?
The hours on the outer ring show morning time (am).
The hours on the inside show afternoon time (pm).
Copy and complete this table from the clock.

Times before noon	1	2	3	4	5	6	7	8	9	10	11	12
Times after noon	13		15			18						

So, instead of showing 3 pm, the railway clock shows 15 hours.
This is written 15.00 hours.
How many hours are there between each pair of times in your table?

2 Simon and John go on a bicycle ride. They start at noon.
The times in this chart are written as hours pm. Copy the chart and rewrite the times using the 24-hour clock.

Event	Time	24-hour clock
Simon has a puncture	1 pm	
They start again	3 pm	
They have a snack	4 pm	
They start home	5 pm	
They arrive home	6.15 pm	

Content
Introducing and using the 24-hour clock for times after midday.

Vocabulary
24-hour clock

Equipment
clocks marked in 24 hours, timetables using 24-hour system, (eg bus, rail, air), classroom clock (12-hour)

Notes
1. Precede by asking the children whether the numbers on all the clocks and watches at home go from 1 to 12. If possible, ask them to bring examples of clocks which use the 24-hour system. Ask them to bring bus, rail and air timetables using the 24-hour system.

2. Focus attention on the method of writing times in the 24-hour style. Hours are written as, for example, 1200 hours. Four

digits are always quoted, so that on the telephone the listener knows when the time stated is complete. For example, 7 am is written as 0700 hours (zero seven hundred hours), but this problem will be dealt with in Level 3.

3. You may find it convenient to make a large 24-hour clock for the classroom.

4. Provide regular practice in converting times of day to the 24-hour system and vice versa. Ask the children to write stories using the 24-hour system.

Q2 Ask the children how long the boys were out on their bicycle ride.

Worksheet 28 provides practice in using am and pm and the 24-hour clock.

Pages 126 and 127 Checkpoint

Content
Checking whether the children can (a) tell and write the time correctly to the nearest five minutes, (b) calculate duration of time, including duration spanning midnight.

Equipment
clocks with moveable hands (the children may need to use these to calculate short durations of time), 2-centimetre squared paper (or if not possible, centimetre squared paper)

Notes
Q1 The times on the clocks, in order, are 7.30, 7.50, 8.05, 9.10, 10.40, 10.55
(a) 20 minutes (b) 15 minutes
(c) 1 hour 5 minutes (d) 30 minutes
(e) 12.30

Q2 2015, 1400, 1045, 1630, 1000, 1900, 1115, 2320

Q3 (a) John goes to bed earliest.
Tom goes to bed latest.
(b) John gets up first.
Clare gets up last.
(c) Clare is in bed longest.
Tom is in bed for the shortest time.

Q4 If available, it is best to use 2-centimetre squared paper. Centimetre squared paper can be used, but the work may be cramped. Remind the children to collect bedtimes etc in whole hours.

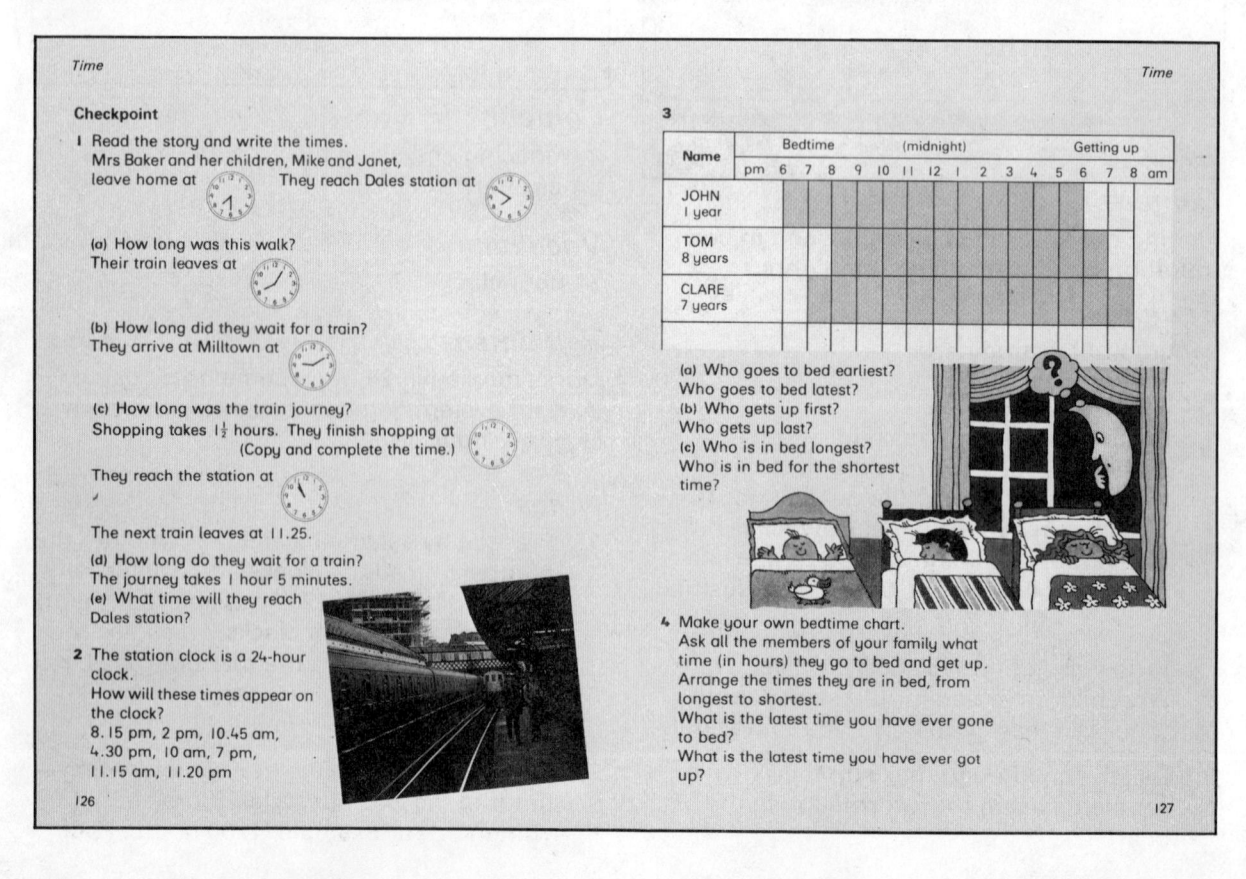

Time

Checkpoint
1 Read the story and write the times.
Mrs Baker and her children, Mike and Janet, leave home at ☐ They reach Dales station at ☐
(a) How long was this walk?
Their train leaves at ☐
(b) How long did they wait for a train?
They arrive at Milltown at ☐
(c) How long was the train journey?
Shopping takes 1½ hours. They finish shopping at ☐ (Copy and complete the time.)
They reach the station at ☐
The next train leaves at 11.25.
(d) How long do they wait for a train?
The journey takes 1 hour 5 minutes.
(e) What time will they reach Dales station?

2 The station clock is a 24-hour clock.
How will these times appear on the clock?
8.15 pm, 2 pm, 10.45 am, 4.30 pm, 10 am, 7 pm, 11.15 am, 11.20 pm

3

Name	Bedtime (midnight) Getting up
JOHN 1 year	pm 6 7 8 9 10 11 12 1 2 3 4 5 6 7 8 am
TOM 8 years	
CLARE 7 years	

(a) Who goes to bed earliest?
Who goes to bed latest?
(b) Who gets up first?
Who gets up last?
(c) Who is in bed longest?
Who is in bed for the shortest time?

4 Make your own bedtime chart.
Ask all the members of your family what time (in hours) they go to bed and get up.
Arrange the times they are in bed, from longest to shortest.
What is the latest time you have ever gone to bed?
What is the latest time you have ever got up?

Worksheets 29–32 provide further numerical practice, mainly in multiplication and division, in the form of puzzles. They can be used at the teacher's discretion at any time after the appropriate work has been done.

Worksheet 29 contains multiplication practice and a number-cross involving the four operations.

Answers

1 (a) 138 (b) 108 (c) 288 (d) 205
  (e) 224 (f) 258
2 108 buns
3 160 marbles
4

a 1	b 2		c 2	d 3
e 1	4	f 4		7
	g 3	9	h 3	
i 2		j 1	2	k 1
l 2	5		m 1	4

Worksheet 30 is a message puzzle which gives practice in finding remainders. There is also a number-pattern question.

Answers

A I like my maths

B 1 15, 21   2 24, 28
   3 24, 42   4 20, 40
   5 7, 14   6 84, 82, 78
   7 63, 54, 36   8 75, 70, 55
   9 63, 57, 54   10 48, 40, 32

Worksheet 31 provides general number practice.

Answers

1 (b) 15 (c) 42 (d) 12 (e) 40 (f) 54 (g) 32
  (h) 30 (i) 36 (j) 21
2 126, 342, 468, 504, 783
3 (a)

3	9	15
12	18	24
21	27	33

(b)

12	19	26
17	24	31
22	29	36

(c)

17	25	33
21	29	37
25	33	41

(d)

35	38	41
29	32	35
23	26	29

(e)

42	33	24
46	37	28
50	41	32

(f)

100	92	84
93	85	77
86	78	70

Worksheet 32 requires multiplication to solve the clues.

Answers

Fish
1 (a) right 1
  (b) up 4
  (c) right 5
  (d) down 2
  (e) left 4
  (f) up 1

Fisherman
2 (a) left 1
  (b) down 5
  (c) left 4
  (d) up 1
  (e) right 1
  (f) up 2

The fisherman does not catch the fish.